ADVANCE PRAISE FOR *E*

"In a legal industry that is poised for massive disruption, all lawyers simply *must* start to think like, behave like, and learn from world-class entrepreneurs. With *Escape the Law*, Chad Williams offers the ideal guide for lawyers who want to move from the traditional path to an entrepreneurial one."

—**VERNE HARNISH**, CEO, Gazelles, Inc.
Founder, Entrepreneurs' Organization
Author, *Scaling Up: Rockefeller Habits 2.0*
Wilmington, Delaware

"Every entrepreneur must have a crystal-clear picture (or 'Vivid Vision') of the future they want to live so they can map out a plan to get there. In *Escape the Law*, Chad Williams provides the motivation and a step by step process for lawyers to create a unique vision of their future as entrepreneurs—both inside the practice of law and out! Read this book, create your own Vivid Vision, and start working!"

—**CAMERON HEROLD**, Author of *Double Double* and
Meetings Suck Founder, COO Alliance
Phoenix, Arizona

"Lawyers are required to pursue continuing education; entrepreneurs are not! Yet every serious entrepreneur is committed to personal and professional development as a way to enhance their performance. If you are a lawyer who has shifted their paradigm from 'just a lawyer' to an entrepreneurial mindset (whether with your practice or outside of it), then *Escape the Law* is the companion you need for your entrepreneurial journey!"

—**JOHN RATLIFF**, Co-Founder and Managing Director, align5, LLC
Founder of Appletree Answers (sold in 2012)
Board Advisor to Virgin Unite
Wilmington, Delaware

"As an NFL veteran and member of the executive committee of the NFL Players' Association, I have participated in a number of business-oriented events and programs. In working with Chad Williams, I have greatly benefited from his ability to take complex subjects and make them understandable and relatable. In *Escape the Law*, Chad does for lawyers what he has done for me and several of my teammates and friends in the NFL: he lays out the path from where you are today to a future in business."

—**MARK HERZLICH**, Author, *What It Takes: Fighting for My Life and the Love of the Game*
2011 Super Bowl XLVI Champion with the New York Giants
Member, Executive Committee, NFL Players' Association
New York, New York

"Drop your buoys, yes—then keep rowing to your next horizon. Chad did just that and learned along the way that he could 'escape' the traditional 'BigLaw' trap and, instead, fulfill his entrepreneurial desire. This book tells Chad's story alongside a dynamic group of 'Alphas,' giving insight into the path for escaping the chains that are potentially holding you from your own greatness."

—**ANDY BAILEY**, Founder of Petra Coach
Author, *No Try, Only Do: Building a Business on Purpose, Alignment and Accountability*
Franklin, Tennessee

"In life, learning on your own path is required; however, learning from the path of others is an art and can take you even further. Read *Escape the Law*, enjoy and grow."

—**ARNIE MALHAM**, Author, *Worth Doing Wrong*;
Serial Entrepreneur: Legal Intake Professionals (sold in 2017)
cj Advertising (sold in 2018)
Betterbookclub.com (growing)
Nashville, Tennessee

"Entrepreneurs look for gaps in the market and build solutions to fill those gaps. There is no shortage of opportunity, but it takes a unique skill set to take something from an idea to execution and exit. Chad Williams has been a great friend and advisor to me as I have built, scaled, and sold my business. With *Escape the Law*, he is sharing his deep insights on what it takes for lawyers to be successful as entrepreneurs. This book will inspire you and provide a clear path for your future in business."

—**ADAM BOALT**, Entrepreneur, Co-Founder,
RushMyPassport.com (sold in 2012) Founder, LiveAnswer (sold in 2016)
Founder, TravelVisa.com (a division of govWorks)
Miami, Florida

"Entrepreneurship can be lonely, and no amount of formal education can prepare you for some of the challenges you face when building a business. As I grew my company, I learned from the experiences of other entrepreneurs, which helped me design solutions and create opportunities of my own. In *Escape the Law*, Chad Williams, a great friend and fantastic advisor, invites you to learn from some of the most successful lawyers-turned-entrepreneurs in history. This book will open your eyes and give you the spark you need to pursue your business interests outside of the practice of law."

—**TOM TURNER**, CEO, DSicovery, LLC (sold to Counsel on Call, 2017)
Nashville, Tennessee

"Being a professional athlete, I have learned to view my brand as a business and I am the chief executive. With that in mind, just as I learn from great football players and coaches, I am committed to learning from entrepreneurs who have reached the top of their game. Chad is a great example of a lawyer and entrepreneur who has reached an elite level of success, and who is also a great teacher. Chad's unique background, diverse experience, and passion for serving others has been invaluable to my personal development and the way I approach business."

—**DEVON KENNARD**, New York Giants
www.devonkennard.com
New York, New York

"Transitioning out of the NFL is similar to the concept of 'living in the gap,' as described in *Escape the Law*. Before I met Chad Williams, I was unable to take a moment to appreciate everything football has given me because I was focused on reaching new goals. Chad helped me realize that by 'dropping buoys' along my quest for brighter horizons, I should never lose sight of goals I've accomplished, while also energizing myself towards my next venture."

—**SPENCER PAYSINGER**, Retired Professional Football Player
(New York Giants, Miami Dolphins)
2011 Super Bowl XLVI Champion with the New York Giants
Entrepreneur, Investor and Screenwriter
Los Angeles, California

"In recent years, world class athletes, artists, and entertainers have vastly improved their abilities to earn success through entrepreneurship. On my podcast, *Suiting Up with Paul Rabil*, I dig deep into the habits, best practices and methods that elite professionals use to leverage the strength of their brands in business. In *Escape the Law*, Chad Williams does a phenomenal job of highlighting compelling stories of dozens of 'Alphas' – former lawyers who made the transition from the practice of law to reach the pinnacle of success as entrepreneurs. This book is *not* for those looking for easy answers or shortcuts, but for the select few who are willing to sacrifice and invest the blood, sweat, and tears it takes to become a world class entrepreneur."

—**PAUL RABIL**, CEO of Rabil Companies;
Founder and Host of *Suiting Up* Podcast;
2017 Most Tech-Savvy Professional Athlete;
Professional Lacrosse Player with the Long Island Lizards;
Member of the United States Men's Lacrosse World Team
Baltimore, Maryland

"Wrestling is a very gritty and cerebral sport that parallels life as well as business. As both a world-class athlete and coach to Olympic wrestlers, I have always been a student of elite performers—seeking to model and synthesize their best strategies and applying them on and off the mat. As Chad Williams convincingly demonstrates in *Escape the Law*, anyone who is willing to be humble, coachable, and learn from elite performers can achieve greatness. Any student of business and world-class performers will enjoy the many relatable stories in this book. Humble yourself, put in the work, give full effort, struggle well, and great things will follow!"

—**BRANDON SLAY**, Executive Director and Head Coach,
Pennsylvania Regional Training Center;
Gold Medalist, Sydney Olympics (2000);
2X All-American and 2X National Finalist in
Wrestling for the University of Pennsylvania;
The Wharton School of Business of the
University of Pennsylvania, Bachelor of Science in Economics,
with a concentration in Entrepreneurial Management
and Finance (1998)
Philadelphia, Pennsylvania

ESCAPE THE LAW

ESCAPE THE LAW

THE JOURNEY FROM LAWYER TO ENTREPRENEUR

CHAD WILLIAMS

NEW YORK

LONDON • NASHVILLE • MELBOURNE • VANCOUVER

ESCAPE THE LAW

The Journey from Lawyer to Entrepreneur

Published in New York, New York, by Morgan James Publishing. Morgan James is a trademark of Morgan James, LLC. www.MorganJamesPublishing.com

The Morgan James Speakers Group can bring authors to your live event. For more information or to book an event visit The Morgan James Speakers Group at www.TheMorganJamesSpeakersGroup.com.

ISBN 9781683508458 paperback
ISBN 9781683508465 eBook
Library of Congress Control Number: 2017917472

Cover Design by:
Emir Orucevic
Pulp Studio

Interior Design by:
Chris Treccani
www.3dogcreative.net

Author Photo by:
Tatum Williams

In an effort to support local communities, raise awareness and funds, Morgan James Publishing donates a percentage of all book sales for the life of each book to Habitat for Humanity Peninsula and Greater Williamsburg.

Get involved today! Visit
www.MorganJamesBuilds.com

For Cara

FOREWORD

eaders are learners—but they don't do it alone. Most have developed the unique ability to learn from the experiences of other successful people, be they personal mentors, coaches, or other leaders, and to adapt this knowledge to their own careers.

It is well documented that top performers in business spend many hours a day consuming information—thinking, analyzing, and synthesizing, rather than simply responding to external conditions. People like Warren Buffet (who reads about five hours a day) and Mark Cuban (who spends at least three hours a day reading) are like miners chipping away at vast blocks of information, gathering bits and pieces they, later, put together in innovative ways.

As chairman and CEO of the global executive education and coaching organization Gazelles Inc. and author of *Scaling Up: Rockefeller Habits 2.0,* my primary role is educating leaders.

Through this work and my experiences founding Entrepreneurs' Organization, I have observed that many lawyers and their firms are grappling with many of the same issues that companies in a multitude of industries are facing today: changes in the economy, new regulations, disruptive technologies, and a transformation in client/market expectations. The very nature of strong, vibrant capitalist economies is that constant competition threatens existing business models. This puts pressure on firms that don't keep pace but also presents fantastic opportunities for those willing to put in the work to get in front of the changes.

Against this backdrop, all lawyers simply *must* start to think like, behave like, and learn from world-class entrepreneurs as a matter of career survival.

These skills are not currently part of legal education in ABA-accredited law schools. You won't be tested on these subjects on any bar exam. You probably will not hear about them in most continuing legal education courses.

Where you will learn them is in *Escape the Law: The Journey from Lawyer to Entrepreneur*. Chad Williams' forward-thinking book is the portal that will carry you from the traditional path that most lawyers have followed for at least the last fifty years to a new world of opportunity.

In *Escape the Law*, Williams shows lawyers how to move from the traditional path to an entrepreneurial one, drawing on the experiences of nearly sixty individuals who earned their law degree before embarking on entrepreneurial paths outside the practice of law. Some, like Charlie Munger, spent years practicing law and even founded their own firm before diversifying into other business interests. Others, like Sam Zell, didn't last very long in the practice of law and, instead, dove headfirst into entrepreneurship during (or shortly after) law school.

I was surprised to learn that more than fifty of the individuals profiled in *Escape the Law* were named among the Forbes 400 wealthiest people in the United States (and many still hold that distinction). None of them earned their immense wealth through the practice of law, which probably won't surprise you if you are a practicing attorney.

Is this to say that money is the only measure of success, or that most lawyers should forsake the practice of law entirely? Absolutely not. Nevertheless, as Williams demonstrates, the very skills and attributes that one must develop in order to be a great lawyer can lead to massive success in business, which ultimately allows attorneys to have an even greater impact on society.

It doesn't take an insider to recognize that the legal services industry is ripe for massive disruption. It is up to you to decide whether you want to lead or simply react to the changes around you. If you are ready to lead, *Escape the Law* is the ideal guide.

Read this book, and then start scaling up!

—VERNE HARNISH

TABLE OF CONTENTS

FOREWORD   xiii

INTRODUCTION   xix

PART ONE: LAYING THE FOUNDATION FOR

A SUCCESSFUL ESCAPE   1

CHAPTER ONE: *I've Done It (Twice), and So Can You!*   3

    The Early Years   4

    My First "Real" Job   5

    The Law School Years   9

    Becoming a Business Lawyer   9

    My First Escape   10

    Failed Attempt   13

    Law Firm Life (Redux)   15

    Making Partner   16

    Overcoming the "Gap" and Planting Seeds   19

    A New Approach   21

    My Great Escape   23

CHAPTER TWO: *Common Alpha Characteristics*   25

PART TWO: THE GREATEST ESCAPES OF ALL TIME   33

CHAPTER THREE: *Titans of Industry*   35

    Sumner Redstone—Viacom Corporation   35

    Riley Bechtel—Bechtel Corporation   37

    Stephen Rales—Danaher Corporation   38

Henry Silverman—Cendant Corporation 40

Michael Jaharis—Kos Pharmaceuticals 42

Randall J. Kirk—New River Pharmaceuticals 43

Robert Rowling—TRT Holdings, Inc. 45

Charlie Munger—Berkshire Hathaway 46

John Anderson—Topa Equities Ltd. 49

Gerald J. Ford—Banking 51

CHAPTER FOUR: *Empire Builders* 55

Sam Zell—Equity Group Investments 56

Richard Lefrak—Lefrak Organization 58

Neil Bluhm—JMB Realty Corp 59

Thomas Barrack—Colony Northstar 61

Bernard F. Saul, II—B.F. Saul Company & Saul Centers, Inc. 64

CHAPTER FIVE: *Allocators of Capital* 67

Reginald Lewis—TLC Beatrice 68

David Rubenstein—Carlyle Group 71

David Bonderman—TPG Capital 72

Jerome Kohlberg and George Roberts—
Kohlberg Kravis & Roberts 73

Teddy Forstmann—Forstmann Little & Company 75

Tully Friedman—Friedman, Fleischman & Lowe 78

Benno Charles Schmidt, Sr.—J.H. Whitney & Company 79

CHAPTER SIX: *Wildcatters* 83

Richard Kinder—Kinder Morgan, Inc. 84

Trevor Rees-Jones—Chief Oil & Gas 86

Joseph Craft, III—Alliance Resource Partners 88

Randa Williams—Enterprise Products 89

CHAPTER SEVEN: *Masters of the Universe* 93

Robert D. Ziff—Ziff Brothers Investments 93

Bruce Karsh—Oaktree Capital Management 95

Paul E. Singer—Elliott Management Corporation 96

Craig Cogut—Pegasus Capital Advisors 97

CHAPTER EIGHT: *In the Arena* 101

Dan Gilbert—Quicken Loans (Cleveland Cavaliers) 101
Stephen Ross—The Related Companies (Miami Dolphins) 103
Ted Lerner—Lerner Enterprises (Washington Nationals) 105
Marc Lasry—Avenue Capital (Milwaukee Bucks) 107
Mark Walter—Guggenheim Partners (L.A. Dodgers) 108
Donald Sterling—Real Estate Investor
(former owner of L.A. Clippers) 109
Lewis Katz—Kinney Parking Systems (New Jersey Nets) 111
CHAPTER NINE: *The New School* 113
Peter Thiel—PayPal, Palantir, Facebook (and more) 114
Todd Wagner—Broadcast.Com 115
Eric Lefkofsky and Brad Keywell—
Starbelly, Groupon (and others) 116
Chris Sacca—Lowercase Capital 118
CHAPTER TEN: *Passion* 121
Leon Charney—L.H. Charney & Associates 122
Mort Zuckerman—Real Estate & Publishing 123
Jim Cramer—Hedge Funds, Author, Television Personality 124
Ron Shapiro—Sports Agent and Author 126
Donald Dell—ProServ 128
Larry Flax & Rick Rosenfield—California Pizza Kitchen 130
Jess Stonestreet Jackson, Jr.—Jackson Family Wines 131
Nina and Tim Zagat—The Zagat Restaurant Surveys 132

PART THREE: ESCAPING THE LAW **137**
CHAPTER ELEVEN: *Define Success* 139
CHAPTER TWELVE: *Escape Planning* 143
CHAPTER THIRTEEN: *For Those Who Remain* 151
CHAPTER FOURTEEN: *Conclusion* 157

ACKNOWLEDGEMENTS 159
ABOUT THE AUTHOR 163

INTRODUCTION

There is a common perception that lawyers make lousy entrepreneurs. In fact, many lawyers seem to accept that the two roles are mutually exclusive. In other words, the day-to-day skills it takes to be a great lawyer are at odds with the qualities one must possess to be a successful entrepreneur.

To a certain extent, this is true. In providing valuable counsel to clients, a lawyer must assess risk and advise accordingly. Many times, this requires drawing attention to possible negative outcomes and worst-case scenarios, and steering clients away from perceived "dangers." Conversely, entrepreneurs must be pathologically optimistic. While successful entrepreneurs don't ignore risk, they also don't let risk stand in the way of opportunity. While this conflict certainly exists, I believe the skills one develops as a lawyer can be fundamental to building a successful business—whether that business be a burgeoning law practice or a billion-dollar company.

This book is the product of many years of hard work, self-directed study, and research into the lives of those who have escaped the practice of law and achieved remarkable success in world of business. I wrote this book to provide hope and inspiration and to encourage bright, hard-working lawyers (and aspiring lawyers) to embrace risk and summon the confidence needed to blaze a trail of their own design. I use the term "escape" to mean an escape from the traditional path lawyers have followed in the practice of law for the last fifty years. Rather than be trapped in the well-trodden path of college, to law school, to associate, to (hopefully) one day becoming a partner in a firm, this book maps out a new path—one where the best lawyers are entrepreneurs that make an impact on the world through law *and* entrepreneurship, by creating jobs, delivering value, and generating wealth.

I fully acknowledge that many people leave the practice of law behind to find success in fields outside of business. Some become teachers and counselors, while others become members of the clergy, politicians, yoga instructors, artists, musicians, or writers. Those are all admirable pursuits, and I commend everyone that takes a leap and reinvents themselves. Happiness and a sense of fulfillment are what life is all about. But this book is about breaking the shackles of the traditional legal profession through entrepreneurship.

I've always admired lawyers who are dedicated to the practice of law and love the work. During my time in the law, I worked with (and across from) lawyers who were passionate about counseling and advocating for their clients and couldn't imagine doing anything else professionally. Lawyers often get a bad rap, but there are fine people out there providing outstanding services and advocacy to their clients—and the business world desperately needs lawyers like that. The business world needs "deal-oriented" lawyers with a win-win approach to negotiation.

While most of the lawyers-turned-entrepreneurs profiled in this book have earned remarkable financial success (in many cases, they have become billionaires), that is not necessarily what I mean by "success" for purposes of this book.

To be sure, we all must pay the bills and prepare financially for the future. Nevertheless, in my experience, decisions made solely or primarily based on the pursuit of financial gain rarely lead to true personal fulfillment. The deeper lesson in this book is about building a successful, fulfilling professional life as an entrepreneur within the practice of law, or entirely outside of it.

The stories that follow demonstrate that if one is not suited to the traditional law firm existence but has a passion for entrepreneurship, they can leverage their legal training and produce fantastic results in business. In my view, the measure of financial success one ultimately earns is a product of one's focus on the process of adding value in the marketplace and finding true professional satisfaction and, most importantly, individual freedom. While many lawyers believe they are trapped with no viable means of escape, my hope is that this book will also give entrepreneurially minded lawyers the confidence and inspiration to overcome that mental obstacle.

For the lawyer currently practicing (or in law school) that feels like a fish out of water, this book is for you. For the lawyer who does the work and even excels, but finds that more success often equals more stress and misery, this book is for you. And this book is for the lawyer who wants a different seat at the table, whose deepest desire is to accomplish great things, and who wants to be happy while doing it.

I know you can earn this outcome in your life. The aim of this book is to give you the confidence and mindset to successfully mount your escape from the traditional practice of law to a new professional life through entrepreneurship.

PART ONE

LAYING THE FOUNDATION FOR A SUCCESSFUL ESCAPE

CHAPTER ONE

I've Done It (Twice), and So Can You!

This book is not about me. I am not yet far enough along in my journey to warrant a "here's how I did it" book, and I have not (yet) achieved the same measure of financial success as the people on the pages that follow. But I have "escaped" the practice of law twice and lived to tell about it. More importantly, each time (including currently), I was immediately happier and found greater professional fulfillment than when I was practicing.

* * *

The image of the perpetually miserable lawyer has become so prevalent that it is now cliché. While we can all picture the curmudgeon lawyer who has been practicing law for thirty years and doesn't intend to stop any time soon, that is not the "miserable lawyer" to which I am referring. A lawyer that's been toiling away, perhaps slavishly chasing the brass ring of partnership; a lawyer that's experiencing the soul-crushing despair that comes with the realization of being trapped in a professional life that is no longer fulfilling; a lawyer that feels resigned, that thinks fate has been sealed and there's no way out—this is the person I am speaking to.

I was one of those lawyers. The first time I felt the urge to leave it was a beautiful Saturday afternoon, early in my legal career. I was stuck in the office, drafting a purchase agreement. I vividly remember looking out the window and thinking, *Why am I always working on someone else's deal, rather than working on a deal of my own?* That's when I decided there had to be another way. I started studying the lives of successful entrepreneurs, with a special focus on lawyers who made the escape from the practice of law to the world of business. The gradual realization that there were others who had done this successfully gave me hope and purpose.

Now, more than a decade later, I have made my second, and final, escape and am on my own entrepreneurial journey. My goal with this book is to share all that I have learned in hopes that it might inspire every lawyer who wants to design an escape plan and get started. Happiness and success through entrepreneurship can be your reality, too. While this book is not about me, for you to understand why I might have something of value to share, here's a bit of my backstory.

THE EARLY YEARS

I was never one of those people who knew they wanted to go to law school from a very young age. I grew up in Coatesville, Pennsylvania, a racially and socioeconomically diverse, blue-collar town about thirty miles west of Philadelphia. Until just after my junior year in high school, I held out hope that I might one day play in the National Football League. My plan was to earn a football scholarship at Penn State, have a fantastic college career, get drafted, and play in the NFL (preferably for my hometown team, the Philadelphia Eagles). Unfortunately, I lacked the size and speed (perhaps not the heart) to play at that level. Nevertheless, I loved athletics and wanted to continue playing in college, and so I focused my college choices on strong academic institutions where I thought I had the best chance of playing.

I chose Franklin & Marshall College (F&M) in Lancaster, Pennsylvania, a small liberal arts college that is well regarded for its rigorous academic standards and grueling workload. I played Division III football and lacrosse and, after a slow start academically, I was eventually a dean's list student. I studied government, English, economics, and business and took advantage of my liberal arts education by exploring numerous other disciplines (such as philosophy, chemistry, astronomy, painting, languages, and history, among other subjects). And yet, as I approached my senior year, I did not know what I wanted to do after graduation. Many of my friends were headed to Wall Street, where some would later find their way to hedge funds and other trading firms, while others were preparing for graduate school (mostly medical and law school). As for me, I wanted to be in business, and so I started to study the accomplishments of people like Bill Gates, Steve Jobs, Richard Branson, Henry Kravis, and others in my free time. Nevertheless, I lacked a clear vision as to how I would enter the business world. I was starting from ground zero.

MY FIRST "REAL" JOB

No one in my family had ever attended graduate school, so as I was approaching my senior year, law school was not on my radar. My father was an entrepreneur and was brilliant when it came to building relationships and representing products in the medical device world. My dad was self-employed for most of my life, and I love and admire him and my mom for their tireless worth ethic, sacrifice, and courage it took to support a family of six without a safety net. As a family, we enjoyed the years of plenty when my father's business was doing well, and endured the lean years when the business hit a rough patch. Yet, we never lacked the essentials and my parents provided my siblings and me a wonderful foundation with fantastic experiences and memories that I will forever cherish.

Having grown up in a blue-collar town, I lacked the connections many of my college classmates had, which seemed to open doors on Wall Street or provide access to other career opportunities. I didn't know anyone at Goldman Sachs, Morgan Stanley, Merrill Lynch, Lehman Brothers, Bear Stearns, or any other Wall Street firms, and so I didn't see a way in where I could demonstrate my value and work my way up the ladder. So, instead, I focused my search on opportunities closer to my hometown in suburban Philadelphia.

In the late 1980s, an entrepreneur named Charlie Cawley took Maryland National Bank, an old-line regional bank, and transformed it into MBNA, a credit card juggernaut and pioneer of a then-unique "affinity marketing" strategy that transformed the consumer lending industry. MBNA was headquartered in Wilmington, Delaware, and the company grew rapidly throughout the late '80s and early '90s.

I earned an internship with MBNA during the summer between my junior and senior year, during which I worked with a group of business analysts who provided management reporting on key performance metrics like delinquency (cardholders behind on payments) and charge-off (cardholders walking away from their obligation to the bank), particularly as it related to the portfolios of credit card loans the bank acquired from other (usually smaller) banks. I liked the culture at MBNA and believed it would be a great place to work after graduation.

Based on my internship experience, MBNA was a true meritocracy. Many people in senior leadership positions did not have Ivy League pedigrees; they were loyal, hardworking, and street smart, and they embodied an esprit de corps that reminded me of the successful athletic teams on which I had played.

During my internship, I sought every opportunity to meet influential managers in order to demonstrate my strong work ethic, willingness to learn, and desire to go above and beyond to contribute to the company's goals. Through those meetings, I learned about MBNA's Management Development Program (MDP)—a program that inducted recent college graduates and, in some cases, military veterans, into an intense, year-long management training rotation through key departments at the bank. After the MDP, participants earned management positions and were fast-tracked to more senior leadership positions.

MBNA reflected the scrappiness of Charlie Cawley, its founder and CEO, and I believed that I was a viable candidate for the program. I applied between my junior and senior year at F&M. MBNA had a rigorous selection process for the MDP. Fortunately, I was granted an interview for the program.

The day-long interview process was with some of the most talented leaders at the bank. I'm hypercritical of my performance in everything I do, but I truly believed that I performed well.

My final interview was with a man named Jack Hewes, one of the top executives at MBNA, and it was the best of the bunch. We hit it off immediately. Like me, Jack came from humble beginnings. He was an athlete and believed that participation in athletics was a strong indicator of success in business, particularly within MBNA's culture.

At the end of my interview, Jack did something that I would later learn was unprecedented in the MDP process. He told me—on the spot—I was exactly the type of person MBNA should have in its MDP, and that he was going to recommend me for the program.

When I returned to campus that fall I was elated. While I wasn't headed to Wall Street like many of my friends, it seemed that I had earned a position in a well-regarded management training program at a rapidly growing, multi-billion-dollar financial institution.

About three weeks into the semester, upon returning to campus after my Saturday afternoon football game, I grabbed the mail on the way into the house. As I was thumbing through letters, postcards, and junk, I noticed an envelope with the distinctive MBNA logo.

My heart raced. I tore it open. In short, after the bank thanked me for my time, they regretted to inform me that I had not been selected for the program. My heart was crushed, and I didn't have a Plan B.

I could not understand how this happened. As I replayed all the interviews in my head, I could not think of any mistake that would have been enough to override Jack's endorsement.

After sulking for a day or two, I decided to take Jack up on his offer to meet when I returned for my internship over winter break.

In early January 1996, I arrived in Jack's cavernous office and sat down across from him. After a few minutes of small talk, and knowing that Jack was a straight shooter, I got to the point. "Jack," I said, my heart racing. "As you may know, I was rejected for the Management Development Program. I was hoping you could share some feedback, so I can understand why I wasn't selected, but, also, so I can learn what to do to be considered for the program in the future."

"Chad," Jack began. "I'm glad you reached out. Most people wouldn't have taken me up on that offer. I guess the title and grey hair make me seem unapproachable. You can apparently decipher between a genuine invitation and a brush off, which is one of the reasons I liked you in the first place."

With that simple response, I was at ease.

Then he waited for what seemed like several minutes before saying, "This place has changed quite a bit over the last few years. Without going into too much detail, there are a limited number of spots in every management development program cohort. And I still think you're a perfect candidate."

I continued to relax as I realized my instincts were right all along.

"But, I'm one guy, and nowadays it seems that everyone at the senior management level is advocating for the son or daughter of a senator, the head of a major association, a trustee at a major university, or the top executives at some major sports team. The nature of our business dictates that oftentimes the candidate with some 'intangible' quality is going to win. I don't like it, but that's the way it is."

In a way, I was relieved, but on the other hand, I was energized by the dismissive nature of the process. If I wasn't good enough for the program because I didn't have anything "intangible" to offer, I would find another way to work my ass off and prove the people who rejected me wrong. As I allowed the implications of what Jack was sharing with me to sink in, the chip on my shoulder grew larger.

Jack continued, "I meant everything I shared with you during your interview, and if you're willing to give MBNA another shot, I'd like to offer you a position in my division."

I could not believe what I was hearing. I came into that meeting half-expecting a brush off, and now I was being offered a job on the spot. Sure, it wasn't the job I wanted, but it was still a solid position in the lending division of the bank, which was on the frontline and provided the lifeblood (i.e., issuing loans from which the bank earned exorbitant interest) for the business.

I accepted Jack's offer and finally had a job lined up following graduation from F&M.

I learned a great deal working at MBNA. But I learned so much more from the process of applying for and being rejected by the Management Development Program, which added fuel to the fire that was already burning in my belly.

THE LAW SCHOOL YEARS

After working in banking for a few years, I applied to a few law schools in the local Philadelphia area and was accepted by Widener University School of Law in Delaware. While Widener lacked the prestige of some of my other choices (Villanova, Temple, etc.), the university offered me a meaningful scholarship. Moreover, it had a solid track record of sending its best students to top corporate law firms in Wilmington, Delaware, which was nationally recognized as the epicenter of business and corporate jurisprudence.

Fortunately, after three years of hard work (during which I was Editor-in-Chief of the nationally recognized *Delaware Journal of Corporate Law*, had a scholarly article published, and was awarded the Outstanding Student Service Award), I graduated with honors and earned a clerkship with Justice Joseph Walsh, then-Senior Justice of the Delaware Supreme Court.

Following my clerkship with Justice Walsh, I accepted a position with the well-regarded corporate law firm Potter Anderson & Corroon LLP, where I had been a summer associate after my 2L year in law school.

BECOMING A BUSINESS LAWYER

I have always admired the careers of entrepreneurs and "business renegades" like T. Boone Pickens and Sir James Goldsmith, and knew I wanted to be a business lawyer. I viewed the practice of law as a way to learn the nuts and bolts of deal-making and negotiating, and figured my lawyer status would earn me a seat at the table. I gained invaluable experience advising business people and negotiating their deals. But the longer I practiced, the more I wanted to build *my own* business and make *my own* deals.

Nevertheless, I continued to grind away at the practice of law for several years before I seized my first opportunity to break out.

It was 2007, and I was working with a great M&A lawyer named Matt Greenberg. Matt spent his formative years at the global behemoth Skadden Arps, and we came together at a Delaware boutique firm called Connolly Bove Lodge & Hutz. Up until that point, I had been very fortunate to learn from some remarkable lawyers (men like Justice Walsh, Mark Morton, Michael Tumas, Mike Pittenger, Mike Reilly, and John Grossbauer, to name just a few), but I really hit my stride with Matt. We worked on all types of deals together, from venture capital financings, to private equity deals, real estate investments, sell-side and buy-side advisory, and complex commercial negotiations (including some nasty business disputes). Matt and I also attended Villanova's LLM tax program together to bolster our knowledge of partnership and other tax matters that were frequently at issue in the deals we handled. We worked well together, and I was incredibly grateful to learn from him.

At that time, Matt was a partner and I was a senior associate. While the boutique nature of Connolly Bove's corporate practice was something that initially drew Matt and me to the firm, we were both growing frustrated with the lack of deep expertise in some key practice areas that we needed to support our growing practice. And then we were presented with a new deal.

MY FIRST ESCAPE

Anyone who has spent any time living or working in Delaware understands that the business and legal communities are small, but powerful. One example of that dual nature was illustrated in the sale of MBNA—yes, the very same bank where I started my career. In January 2006, Bank of America acquired MBNA for more than $34 billion and, as a result of that transaction, Delaware was suddenly home to many newly minted multi-millionaires. As with many mergers of that size, often the people at the top of the acquired company do not remain with the acquirer. And so, in 2006 and 2007, most of those newly minted MBNA millionaires were contemplating their next move.

It was around this time that Matt and I started to work with Shane Flynn (an Irishman who had been the Chief Executive Officer of MBNA Europe) and Frank McKelvey (a Vice Chairman at the time of the Bank of America acquisition). Shane and Frank, along with two of their colleagues from MBNA (Navroze Eduljee, a marketing technology expert, and Blaine Buck, an engineer and large-scale facilities developer) came together to form a private investment firm called Cordjia (pronounced Cord-JA, which is the translation of an Irish expression "a chairde," which means "friends"). Cordjia's objective was to find opportunistic acquisition targets, where the partners could bring capital and their collective experience (gained from many years holding key positions in a multi-billion-dollar company).

Cordjia hired us to help with everything from the formation of their operating and investment entities, to evaluating their early acquisition targets. After a few months, Cordjia landed on two target companies—Goliath Solutions (a marketing technology services company focused on the consumer retail market) and 4tell Solutions (a SaaS company that had developed a multifaceted software platform for owners of commercial real estate).

We worked very closely with the Cordjia team and developed a great business and personal relationship with the principals. Indeed, shortly after closing their first two investments, Cordjia took space one floor above our offices. The Cordjia team had aggressive goals to grow and invest, and Matt and I were well positioned to advise and grow with them.

By the end of 2007, Matt was ready to make a move from our boutique firm, and he was willing to take me with him.

I had some tough decisions to make. I liked and respected Matt, and had fun working with him, and strongly considered moving with Matt. But once Matt's partners knew he was intending to leave, several pitched me on the idea of staying on to lead the growth of the transactional practice for the firm. I was flattered by their confidence in me, and I truly respected the people at Connolly Bove, but I saw this as an opportunity to develop something of my own.

I considered starting my own firm. I plotted out my clients and contacts, put together a pro forma business plan, and seriously considered hanging my own shingle. However, my consideration of that approach was colored by the issues Matt and I had grappled with at Connolly Bove—if I started my own firm, would my ability to provide service to my clients in areas outside my expertise (such as intellectual property, labor and employment, litigation, etc.)

be hindered and ultimately limit my ability to grow my practice, especially as my clients grew and their needs became more varied and complex?[1]

Finally, I thought about the relationships I had developed at Cordjia and asked Matt if he would mind me speaking with the Cordjia principals about joining them in a dual business/legal capacity. To his credit, Matt gave me his blessing.

I met with Frank McKelvey, one of the four original partners at Cordjia. Over the next few weeks, Frank and I negotiated a compensation and equity package. I had successfully made my first transition from the "traditional" law firm world to the world of business (in this case, a small private equity firm).

Psychologically, I wasn't ready to completely cut the cord as a lawyer. For that reason, I would take on the General Counsel role at Cordjia, but I would also be Vice President of Business Development. In my business development role, my responsibilities were to source, evaluate, and lead the negotiation on new investment and other business opportunities for the company and then, once acquired, work directly through the board and with senior management to grow those companies.

As for Matt, he ended up transitioning his practice to Pepper Hamilton and we continued to work together during my time with Cordjia and after. Matt remains a good friend and mentor, and is a world-class deal lawyer.

As 2008 began, I could not have been happier in my new role. I saw so much opportunity ahead, and as our team at Cordjia started to gel, we had some fantastic prospects—both on the investment side, as well as some independent development projects that had a great deal of potential. Unfortunately, that period of professional bliss was short-lived.

FAILED ATTEMPT

The first sign of trouble did not seem like a harbinger of terrible things to come. When Bear Stearns collapsed in March 2008, it was big news if

---

1   Incidentally, if I were considering this issue now, I would probably be less concerned about this. With the growth in technology, as well as new modes of thinking among entrepreneurial lawyers, I believe that business lawyers can augment their teams through other niche-focused boutique firms to provide a broader set of expertise to their core clients. More on this later.

for no other reason than Bear Stearns had been one of the longest-surviving independent investment firms on Wall Street. I had friends from college who had worked at Bear, and I felt badly for them and their families. But the world that Bear Stearns played in was so far from what we were focused on at Cordjia that it did not throw us off our stride.

By early September 2008, however, everything changed. It was then that Lehman Brothers, another Wall Street stalwart, filed for bankruptcy protection in what seemed like the blink of an eye. I had followed the dramatic lead up to the collapse in the *Wall Street Journal*—culminating in an intense weekend showdown between the leaders of major Wall Street institutions and key government officials—and I knew that this was a terrible sign of a much larger financial crisis that would affect our entire economy. As details emerged about the abysmal lending practices in the consumer real estate markets, and then the securitization and trading of those mortgage loans, it was clear the tentacles of this crisis would be far reaching and, in myriad indirect ways, have a direct impact on our business at Cordjia.

It didn't take long. The first crack was our investment in Goliath Solutions. When we invested in Goliath (perhaps the name should have given us pause!), it had just completed a very successful pilot in 1,000 Walgreens stores demonstrating the distinct value of its RFID technology that allowed retailers and consumer packaged goods (CPG) companies to obtain critical insights and analytics into the ROI generated through certain marketing campaigns. And, we were in the process of negotiating similar pilot projects with CVS and other chain drug stores, with the goal of moving on to "big box" and other retailers. The business model would generate significant recurring revenue and result in sticky relationships with both the CPGs and retailers.

Unfortunately, as the broader economy fell into recession in late 2008 and 2009, CPGs aggressively pulled back on their marketing campaigns, thus drastically altering Goliath's revenue forecast.

After fighting for several years to steer the company into calmer waters and back on a path to growth, we simply ran out of time and capital. Our investment in Goliath was an unfortunate, but not uncommon, casualty of the Great Recession. The company had a unique offering that delivered great value to its clients (the CPGs and retailers), but we were simply too badly beaten to recover once the storm had passed.

Our second investment, 4tell Solutions, was performing slightly better, but still suffered from the broader market issues caused by the Great Recession. It lasted a few years longer than our investment in Goliath, and by the time we sold the company we earned what amounted to a return of our invested capital and the payment of management fees that had been deferred for several years. The outcome was not what we had hoped for, but we made our investors whole (including my wife and me, as we had made an additional investment from our personal funds above our share of the carry through Cordjia) and thus it was not a terrible outcome.

During that time, we also internally seeded a software company that developed a cloud-based enterprise resource planning (ERP) software platform targeted toward the marine industry (i.e., custom boat builders and service yards), and a custom, enterprise-level software development practice, both of which are still in operation today. Our ERP solution (called PierVantage) is used by some of the best boat builders and marinas in the country, as well as several impressive international players.

As I told my wife often during that period of my career, those days were incredibly stressful, but professionally rewarding and a lot of fun. The stakes were high. I had personally walked away from a promising legal career with a plan to make my way in business, and I had also invested my personal capital. Unfortunately, by late 2009, it was in the best interests of all of us to wind-up the business, ride out our investments (again, which we ultimately lost with Goliath, and sold with 4tell) and spin the software businesses out into an independent entity (which is still in operation today).

LAW FIRM LIFE (REDUX)

By early 2010, I was managing the process of winding-up Cordjia, while simultaneously considering my next move. Our run at Cordjia hadn't been long enough to truly open up meaningful opportunities as general counsel of another private equity firm, nor was my experience outside of law broad enough at that point to join a private equity group in an investment capacity.

Moreover, many of those firms were suffering through the same issues we faced at Cordjia, and so few firms were looking to add new people—many were just trying to hang on themselves!

With a family of six (my wife, our four children, and myself), the most logical move was to go back into the practice of law. First, I dusted off my business model for opening my own firm. I was confident I could quickly rebuild my practice. But I was still nagged by the (perhaps irrational) concern that I would eventually lose some of those clients if I was unable to offer them expertise in areas such as intellectual property, tax, and other critical legal disciplines. With the benefit of hindsight, I could have added those practice areas to my firm as the need arose or augmented my firm through relationships with other boutique law firms outside my specific niche. On the heels of the financial stress caused by the Great Recession, however, I was looking for something with more stability.

The next rational option was to attempt to re-enter the "large firm" world. I was confident in my ability to build and scale a business practice within such a firm, and so I focused on firms with offices in multiple states, including Pennsylvania, New Jersey, and Delaware, where most of my clients were located. After multiple meetings and interviews, I narrowed my options down to three firms: Pepper Hamilton (back with my old friend, Matt Greenberg), Ballard Spahr (a well-regarded, old-line Philadelphia firm that also had an office in Wilmington), and Saul Ewing (a growing AmLaw 200 firm that was perhaps better known for its litigation and real estate practices, but that had some outstanding lawyers and a core group of entrepreneurially minded leaders in its Business and Finance group).

I joined Saul Ewing, working out of both the Philadelphia and Wilmington offices. The then-Chair of the Business and Finance Department, Barry Levin, offered me a position as Special Counsel, which came with the expectation that I would grow my own practice and have an opportunity to be considered for partnership. I delivered on that expectation and, within two years, built a practice that was rapidly approaching seven figures. Over time, I also accepted multiple firm management and leadership positions (including the hiring committee, director of the summer associate program, Vice Chair of the Business and Finance Department, Co-Chair of our Venture Capital and Private Equity practice group and founding member, and eventually Chair of our Family Enterprise practice group, serving very large family offices and family businesses, which had become a significant focus of my practice). I had also developed a niche working with technology companies and companies in several other industries that were rapidly scaling their respective businesses.

I was growing a profitable law practice, building a team to support that growth, earning a great living (by any reasonable measure), was likely to earn partnership, and was on a leadership path that could potentially lead to a senior leadership position in the firm. Yet for some reason, the more success I earned professionally, the more miserable I was personally.

MAKING PARTNER

I have never been afraid of hard work. In fact, I thrive on it. Throughout my legal career, there were plenty of all-nighters (some that lasted several days in a row), plenty of times that I worked for months at a time without taking a day off, and countless vacations where I found myself in our hotel or vacation house grinding away while my family was out enjoying themselves without me.

While there were times that I was resentful, I also took tremendous pride in the quality of my work and the sacrifices I made for my clients. However, there came a very distinct point where I realized that my addiction to work was not healthy and was incredibly irrational. Unfortunately, it culminated in a week-long stay in the hospital.

Early in my career, as I was building my legal practice, I connected with a company called Appletree Answers, a high-touch call center company based in Wilmington, Delaware and led by a young entrepreneur named John Ratliff. Initially, I helped Appletree with some simple contracts, and our relationship grew from there—I also got to know and work with Ralph Cetrulo, a CPA and partner in Appletree, and Denise Richmond, the company's controller and CFO.

I truly admired John and the Appletree team, and while they were not my largest client, the company represented my longest-tenured and deepest client relationship.

In late 2011, John told me that he was preparing to sell his company. The business was rapidly growing, and he had built a senior management team that could completely run the day-to-day operation of the business, while John provided the strategic vision.

John hired a boutique investment bank to run a strategic process and ultimately accepted an offer from Stericycle Communication Solutions (a division of a public company based in Chicago) at a premium valuation. It was a fantastic outcome for John and for Stericycle, as it acquired a remarkable company that would become its platform for additional growth in that market. It was truly a win-win deal.

At one point during the negotiation, just weeks away from closing, I became severely ill with what I thought was a vicious stomach flu. I could not keep any food or water down for two or three days, I was getting very little sleep, and was in constant pain. Nevertheless, this deal was huge for me, as it involved my most important client (and people I considered my friends), and I was also being considered for partner. Much to my wife's consternation, I would drag myself out of bed each morning, try (unsuccessfully) to keep food and water down, and then head into the office to manage the process and negotiate the deal. Then, on a Saturday morning, after at least two days of a severe illness, I got in my car and started the near-two-hour drive to Baltimore for a strategic planning session for our Business and Finance Department.

I was doubled over in pain during the entire drive and periodically took sips of water along the way. Thirty minutes away from my destination, I pulled over and vomited every ounce of water I had drunk. It finally dawned on me that I might be in real trouble—a ruptured appendix or something more serious.

I drove myself to a hospital closer to home, thinking that if I had to have my appendix removed, I didn't want my wife to have to drive to Baltimore to see me. The admitting nurses could see the seriousness of my condition and they immediately moved me to a treatment room. The nurses performed a battery of tests and exams, hooked me up to IVs, and took other steps to stem my excruciating pain and other symptoms.

After an hour or so, I received the preliminary diagnosis: acute renal (kidney) failure. Had I not arrived at the hospital when I did, my condition (and prognosis) would have been far worse. Essentially, the stomach flu, or whatever it was that caused my inability to keep food and water down for several days, caused severe dehydration. Consequently, my kidneys were failing. I was admitted to the hospital, and the nurses and doctors worked to reverse the damage I had done to my kidneys. Unfortunately, other than the IV fluids, I still could not keep food or water down, and was then experiencing excruciating, migraine-like headaches. I was in bad shape.

By Sunday, I had let a few of my colleagues know what was going on, along with John and the rest of the Appletree deal team. John told me to forget about the deal and get healthy. He reassured me the rest of the team at Saul Ewing would step up and the deal would be fine.

While I knew that John and my colleagues were totally sincere in their admonition to forget about work, I simply couldn't. This was a huge deal for John, and I wanted to personally ensure that everything was done right. I *wanted* to be involved. I *wanted* to be on every call. I *wanted* to review every turn of the documents. Therefore, against the advice of just about everyone who loved and cared for me, I grabbed my laptop and my phone and I was back to work (from my hospital bed) by Monday morning.

I spent almost a week in the hospital before my kidney levels returned to normal and I could keep solids and liquids down. I worked almost the entire time I was there. And, as embarrassing as this is to say, I was proud of it. I still am. It was important to me that John and the Appletree team knew I would do anything I could to help them get the deal done. And I wanted my colleagues at Saul Ewing to know just how committed I was representing our clients' interests and building a successful practice.

As I retell this story now, I realize how ridiculous it sounds, except perhaps to the many lawyers reading this who have similar stories of their own— recovering from a heart attack, serious injury, or childbirth, and getting back to work as soon as an internet connection could be established.

The Appletree deal closed in May 2012. In December 2012, I was named partner at Saul Ewing. In a little more than two years, I had successfully re-entered the practice of law, built a rapidly growing, seven-figure personal practice, and earned partnership in a prestigious Philadelphia law firm. I had achieved goals and accomplished things that many lawyers strive for yet never achieve. Yet, after the initial glow subsided (maybe a month later), things still didn't seem quite right.

OVERCOMING THE "GAP" AND PLANTING SEEDS

Having worked at different law firms, and having once "escaped" law for the business world, I could not understand why I was so unhappy and depressed. As a person of deep faith, I was angry with myself for not being more grateful for, and content with, all my blessings. I started to realize that more work and more "success" was never going to satisfy me. I was nagged by the fact that there were many people where I grew up who toiled away at physically demanding jobs, earning far less than me, who could only dream about having the material blessings I had earned. Yet, despite being thankful for my blessings and proud of the work I had done to get there, I could not deny the fact that I was not happy. In truth, the more successful I became in the practice of law, the more miserable I was.

Meanwhile, a few months had passed since becoming a partner at Saul Ewing, and my practice continued to thrive. I was still working with John Ratliff, helping him structure his family office and close some personal investments. One night, in the spring of 2013, John and I connected for dinner to catch up. It was the first time the two of us had sat down outside of the office and connected on life post the sale of Appletree.

John had just returned from Necker Island, Richard Branson's private island resort in the British Virgin Islands, and he shared some beautiful pictures from his trip (John does work with Virgin's charitable arm, Virgin Unite, and he and Richard are now good friends). John was tanned, lean, and happy, and he asked how I was doing—personally and professionally. I hadn't shared with anyone (other than my wife) the fact that I was depressed and unhappy professionally, but John's relaxed attitude gave me the confidence to open up to him.

John listened patiently as I explained to him that while I had achieved so many professional goals I had set for myself many years ago, I was in this strange spiral where the more success I achieved, the less happy I was. John smiled, took a sip of his beer and said, "You're living in 'the gap!'" I wasn't sure what he meant, but he went on, "This happens to entrepreneurs and high achievers all the time. My business coach, Dan Sullivan, describes it as 'living in the gap.'"

John explained, "Dan has observed that the reason people like us feel empty even after achieving massive goals is that we live in the 'gap' between our present circumstances and the 'horizon,' which represents the new goals and ideals that we set for ourselves almost immediately after we accomplish our current goals. If our 'ideal' state is always at some point in the future—in other words, on some distant horizon—then just as one who walks from the beach into the ocean with the intention of reaching the horizon will never get there, those of us who are driven, goal-oriented people will *never* reach our ideal state—i.e., the horizon—because it is always moving."

The moral of this story was, if we fail to celebrate or drop "buoys" each time we accomplish something big, and then periodically turn around and acknowledge how far we have come, we will never find true peace or contentment in anything we do.

For the first time in years, I heard something that perfectly articulated everything I was feeling. I was absolutely living in the gap, and had been for most of my life. I had never taken the time to turn around and consider how far I had come—from a kid in a diverse blue-collar steel town in southeastern Pennsylvania, to a partner in a top Philadelphia law firm. I had never truly considered the obstacles I had overcome to achieve so many of my goals. The purpose of the exercise was not to pat myself on the back, but rather to personally acknowledge the accomplishments, find gratitude for the journey, and attain peace in my present circumstances.

As dinner continued, and now with a fresh new wave of positive energy, our conversation moved on to what was next for both of us. John shared with me that he wanted to leverage his strategic thinking and negotiation skills to help other entrepreneurs maximize value when they sold their companies. John also shared that he would always be passionate about entrepreneurship and would eventually want to start, acquire, and build another company.

John asked me about my plans for building my practice. I shared with him my success building a robust book of business with middle-market companies and that I fully expected my practice to continue to grow exponentially. But I also told John that my long-term plan was to start to make investments outside of it as part of my greater goal to create multiple sources of income and then eventually transition away from the practice of law to manage my own business interests on a full-time basis. I never wanted to formally "retire" from anything, but rather I sought absolute personal and financial freedom to live a life of my own design as soon as I possibly could.

As we left dinner that night, John and I agreed that there would be an opportunity to do something together in the future. Neither of us knew what that would look like at the time, but as we shook hands and walked away, I was reenergized by the clarity provided by understanding the "gap." I felt invigorated with the prospect of plotting my escape, while continuing to build my practice along the way.

A NEW APPROACH

Over the next year or so, as I continued to build my practice and accept more leadership responsibility within the firm, I redoubled my efforts to plan my business interests outside of my law practice. If I couldn't leave the practice of law entirely, there was nothing stopping me from investing (if only small amounts at first) in myself and in other business pursuits. I studied real estate investing, and I leveraged my experience with technology companies and other growth businesses to analyze other investment opportunities.

Outside of my business life, I enjoyed coaching my kids in their sports, and I tried to fit in as much physical activity as I could. I played tennis in a Tuesday night group with some guys at the country club we belonged to. It was there I met an entrepreneur named Will Snook, which opened up another great new opportunity.

Will was a former pilot who, after a few years flying for a commercial airline, started a business brokering the sale of private aircraft. Unfortunately, following the tragic events of September 11, 2001, sales of private planes came to a grinding halt. With a young family, Will was in search of a new opportunity when his father (a retired DuPont executive) suggested that Will take over a small side business his father was running, selling parking blocks made from recycled materials.

While it took some convincing, Will jumped in, eventually acquired the company from his father and expanded the business. He brought on new products (traffic cones, speed bumps, reflective vests, and other safety products) and invested in building a proprietary online e-commerce platform. Will slowly and steadily built the business over the next ten years or so, but when we met, the business had plateaued and Will was personally burnt out.

Will and I would talk business after our Tuesday night tennis matches, and I would share some thoughts and ideas about growth strategies based on my experience with other growth companies throughout the years.

After a few months of informally meeting with Will to learn about his business, I saw a company that was poised to scale and that had considerable upside opportunity. In August 2013, Will and I agreed to a more formal strategic advisory arrangement. I would work with him on an ongoing basis (in a quasi-director role) in exchange for a modest consulting fee and an opportunity to participate in helping Will design the perfect exit at some point in the future. As I write this book, we've been working together for almost five years and, as a direct result of Will's leadership and the fantastic work of the executive team he has put together, Traffic Safety Store has doubled in size every two years, and has been named to the Inc. 5000 list multiple times.

Based on the early success of my first independent venture outside of my legal practice, I was eager to find the next opportunity. But as my practice continued to grow, my work with Will continued, and my leadership responsibilities at the firm increased, I found it difficult to find the time to look for and analyze new opportunities. It became clear that if I was to execute my law firm/business investments strategy, it would be a marathon, not a sprint.

By the end of 2014, while I had become a full equity partner in the law firm, I was still unhappy. I poured everything I had into deal after deal for my clients, and with every closing wished more and more that I was building a business outside the practice of law. In addition, given the dynamics of a large law firm, my compensation (while terrific and steadily growing) was not what I thought it could be if I were on my own. I watched as the firm's executive committee offered comparable (and in some cases, higher) compensation and profit share packages to certain peers who were far less productive than me, but who brought certain "intangibles" to the firm (such as racial and gender diversity), which were important to win or retain the business of certain key clients. For at least the second time in my life, I found myself in an environment that valued intangibles I did not possess and had no way of acquiring, no matter how hard I worked. While I understood the value those qualities brought to law firms (particularly large firms whose clients demanded such initiatives), I also knew that I was not personally cut out for any bureaucratic environment that placed greater value on intangibles than on merit.

Taking all of this together, I realized that I would never truly be happy or fulfilled until I either started my own firm, or made a clean escape from the practice of law. I truly needed to control my own destiny. Fortunately, a seed that had been planted years before was about to sprout.

MY GREAT ESCAPE

In early 2015, John Ratliff and I connected to discuss some great opportunities that he was pursuing. Given John's deep experience with acquisitions (specifically on the buy side, through his roll-up with Appletree), his passion for working with entrepreneurs on strategy, and my deep experience advising entrepreneurs and negotiating transactions, John and I decided to form a boutique investment banking advisory practice.

In addition to our focus on sell-side M&A engagements in the United States with enterprise values ranging from $50 million up to $500 million, we would also advise entrepreneurs at all stages along the entrepreneurial company lifecycle to help them reach their goals.

I was thrilled to have the opportunity to leverage my network and deep expertise in M&A for the benefit of entrepreneurs and business owners to help them maximize value upon exit. While I would be giving up the virtual "sure thing" of sharing in the profits of a large Philadelphia law firm, I was intrigued by the upside of this new venture and by the ability to be part of building something from the ground up.

After contemplation, prayer and deep discussions with trusted friends (including my wife), I decided that the opportunity was well worth the sacrifice, investment, and risk. I notified my partners that I would be pulling out my equity interest in the firm and spending the next month or so transitioning my client relationships over to a few of my partners. I had escaped the path of a traditional "big firm" lawyer again, and this time, I had no intention of going back.

Once I found myself on the other side of the wall, I realized that there are many others like me looking for a way out. On the pages that follow, I share the profiles of some of the people who gave me the confidence to make my escape.

CHAPTER TWO
Common Alpha Characteristics

H aving studied nearly sixty lawyers-turned-entrepreneurs (whom I will refer to throughout the remainder of the book as "Alphas"), I see certain characteristics that indicate both the likelihood of escape and the likelihood of success in business thereafter. The profiles you will read throughout this book are primarily focused on former lawyers (or people who earned a law degree) who later became multi-millionaires or, in many cases, billionaires. But for every Alpha profiled in this book, there are many more people who have also successfully made the "escape" from law to business with perhaps more modest financial gain or less publicity.

As a practical matter, I focused my research on Alphas because their stories provide tremendous illustrations of what is possible (even if at the margin) for those who make the decision to leverage their skills in the world of business. There is much to be gleaned from the diversity of their backgrounds, their experiences, and the disciplines from which they emerged.

The reader will observe that there is very little racial or gender diversity among the Alphas. As I wrote this book, I spent a considerable amount of time trying to find comparable examples of women and minorities who fit the Alpha model, but I was only able to identify two women and one African American who had accomplished similar levels of success. The story of the one African American Alpha (a man named Reginald Lewis) is my favorite, and one of the most personally relatable, profiles among the Alphas I have studied.

My research is by no means scientific, so I do not believe any broader observations can (or should) be drawn from the apparent lack of diversity among Alphas. Rather, I think there are probably many examples of women and minority lawyers who have "escaped" the practice of law and are very successful in business, just on a more modest scale. (Perhaps instead of billions or hundreds of millions, they are mere millionaires!) Moreover, I believe that diversity among the Alpha group is likely to increase over the next ten to twenty years as greater numbers of women and minority lawyers are represented in the profession and a certain percentage of those lawyers escape the practice of law and achieve notable entrepreneurial success.

COMMON ALPHA CHARACTERISTICS

There are several themes and character traits that you will observe among the Alphas we study in the pages that follow. Specifically, I believe that the Alphas you will read about share several (if not all) of the following, which we will refer to from this point on as "Alpha Characteristics":

1. *They have working-class roots and tight-knit families.* While a few Alphas were born into wealthy families and started with a leg up in life, the overwhelming majority of Alphas have working class roots and, in some cases, grew up extremely poor. Nevertheless, virtually all the Alphas have tight-knit extended families from which they developed the qualities of character (such as a strong work ethic) that laid the foundation for future business success. In several instances, Alphas took over existing family enterprises, created new family enterprises by bringing siblings or children into the business, and learned valuable lessons from certain family members who were engaged in businesses of their own. Unfortunately, in a few sad cases, diverging interests led to heartbreaking rifts between members of the same family. Nevertheless, a common thread that joins the

overwhelming majority of Alphas together is a humble beginning and a focus on family.

2. *They pursued entrepreneurial endeavors early in their lives.* In many cases, Alphas demonstrated an early interest in entrepreneurship and business. Indeed, while some Alphas were born into entrepreneurial families and earned early experience in a family business, others started businesses on their own from a very early age. Some continued to operate their businesses while pursuing their education.

3. *They have a guiding ideology that transcends business and material gain.* A statistically significant number of Alphas were born into Jewish families. In many of those cases, their Jewish heritage and faith seems to play a varying role in the opportunities and pursuits that lead them from law into business. Another interesting personal characteristic among Alphas is that a slim majority are self-identified as conservative/Republicans, while a significant minority identify as either libertarian or liberal/Democrats. Regardless of political ideology, in almost all cases, Alphas generously support causes and people that they believe helped them on their path to success, helping others do the same. Moreover, as one searches more broadly beyond our Alpha subgroup, I believe you will find a strong, guiding faith (be it Jewish, Christian, Muslim, or otherwise) and a clearly articulated and overarching political philosophy. In other words, a common characteristic among Alphas is that they are driven by an ideology that transcends materialism, and that ideology undergirds nearly all the decisions they make in their business and personal lives.

4. *They tested and developed their character through challenges outside of business.* A significant number of Alphas served in the military (mostly during World War II), with duties ranging from the front line to intelligence and administrative roles. In addition, many Alphas were very accomplished athletes at youth and collegiate levels, and in one instance, at the professional level. In those cases, it seems that these experiences in adolescence and early adulthood helped develop

certain aspects of character that later contributed to the success those individuals earned in law and business.

5. *In most cases, academic pedigree mattered very little to their success.* While several Alphas attended Ivy League or similarly prestigious universities, a statistically significant number of Alphas attended state and local universities or smaller private colleges that were close to home or that offered opportunities unavailable elsewhere. The bottom line is, while it certainly has not hurt those Alphas who possess a prestigious academic background, it is not a prerequisite to successfully make the leap from law and earn massive success in business. One could even argue that beyond the Alpha subgroup, those with more modest academic backgrounds might be more willing to take greater risk to jump from the safety, security, and respectability of the law firm world into the scrappier world of entrepreneurship and business.

6. *Pursuit of money is not the primary driver, but nearly all of them are incredibly generous with the wealth they create.* With respect to nearly every Alpha profiled in this book, the pursuit of more money was not the primary impetus to escape the practice of law. In many cases, Alphas who practiced law for more than a few years were leaving behind the certainty of lucrative legal practices for the uncertainty of entrepreneurial endeavors. Rather than greater financial gain, it seems that most Alphas are motivated by the prospect of creating and adding value in the marketplace, producing returns, having fun, and (perhaps most importantly) earning individual freedom. Finally, it is also important to note that while virtually all Alphas eventually earned immense wealth, they have also been incredibly generous with their bounty by funding hospitals, academic institutions, religious causes, and myriad other charitable, social, and political organizations (which ties back to the observation above that many Alphas seem to be driven by an underlying faith and/or political ideology that guides their decisions). Therefore, while the pursuit of money does not appear to be the driving force behind an Alpha's escape from

the practice of law, sincere generosity is a defining characteristic of Alphas who achieve massive success in business.

7. *They have a high tolerance for risk.* As with most businesses, success for Alphas did not come in a straight, upward line, and many of them took enormous risks at various stages of their business lives. Contrary to the common notion that lawyers are risk averse by nature, it seems clear that the legal training possessed by Alphas is critical to their analysis and management of risk.

8. *Most practice law for at least a few years, and some start their own law firms.* Of the nearly sixty Alphas profiled in this book, a few went straight from law school into the business world, and some started their first entrepreneurial ventures before they even graduated. Most, however, practiced law for at least a few years, either in government or private practice, before making their escape, while several practiced for a decade or more before formally exiting the practice of law in favor of their business interests. Among those who practiced for more than a handful of years, several became partners with prestigious law firms, while others started law firms of their own. While many Alphas practiced in transactional practice areas (business, real estate, energy, and bankruptcy), others were successful trial attorneys in practices as diverse as criminal law and personal injury. As will become evident from many of the profiles in later chapters, most Alphas discover early on in their careers that they are not cut out for the traditional law firm environment and therefore plot their escape as soon as they can.

9. *They have diverse experiences inside and outside the practice of law.* As noted earlier, the range of practice areas in which Alphas practiced include business, tax, real estate, energy, bankruptcy, criminal, and personal injury, among others. In many of those cases, the Alphas entered their chosen practice area based on relationships or opportunities that presented themselves early on in their professional careers. In addition, many Alphas brought diverse experience to the practice of law and their entrepreneurial pursuits. From very early ages, they did everything from developing and growing newspaper

routes to selling things like pizza, popcorn, residential real estate, and motorcycles. One Alpha sang in his synagogue to earn money for school, and several others developed unique skills through their service in the military. As they developed experience as entrepreneurs, they seized opportunities to broaden their skills, which then served as the building blocks to reach Alpha status in most cases many years after developing those various skills. Diversity of experience and starting as early as possible provides Alphas with the confidence to accept the circuitous route one must take to achieve success as an entrepreneur. Moreover, based on the diversity of their experience, as these individuals reach Alpha status, they often successfully transition into new areas of business, like the ownership of professional sports teams, writing, and entertainment production.

10. *They overcome adversity and play the long game.* A large segment of our society believes that people who achieve massive financial success were born on third base, believe they hit a triple and followed an all-too-easy path to immense wealth. Of course, this is a gross mischaracterization of the sacrifices made by many self-made billionaires and multi-millionaires, who often rise out of very challenging circumstances before they reach the mountaintop. Most entrepreneurs who achieve any level of success in business have worked extremely hard and in the process of earning their success have improved the lives of countless others along the way. Among the Alphas profiled in this book, most have demonstrated an ability to overcome significant obstacles on their path to success, such as the death of a parent, sibling, or child; job loss; personal bankruptcy; poor business decisions; or a bitter family squabble. Yet, as author Ryan Holiday chronicled in his bestselling book *The Obstacle Is the Way*, highly successful people tend to blaze the path to success by embracing obstacles and finding creative ways to turn them to their advantage.

* * *

Throughout the remainder of this book, we explore the lives and success of Alphas in a variety of industries, including entertainment, marketing, pharmaceuticals, conglomerates, banking, real estate, private equity, venture capital, hedge funds, restaurants, publishing, and professional sports, among others. As you read on, you will note that Alphas possess many (if not all) of the characteristics highlighted above. Through the profiles that follow, you will derive consistent themes, experiences, and attributes that can be synthesized and adapted to develop your own unique escape from the traditional practice of law.

PART TWO

THE GREATEST ESCAPES OF ALL TIME

CHAPTER THREE
Titans of Industry

———

n this chapter, we explore the lives of ten men who took different paths into and through the practice of law and emerged as titans of various industries, including entertainment, construction, banking, pharmaceuticals, and diversified conglomerates. In several cases, these businesses started as (or later became) family businesses. In others, Alphas leveraged early success and doubled down in their industry of choice on their way to building highly successful enterprises. In each case, however, these titans of industry drew on their Alpha Characteristics to create a vision of their business future and to go after it with everything at their disposal.

SUMNER REDSTONE—VIACOM CORPORATION

Sumner Redstone, the chairman and majority shareholder of the National Amusements theater chain, is perhaps best known as the owner of Viacom and CBS Corporation. Redstone was born Sumner Murray Rothstein, but his father later changed the family surname to Redstone at young Sumner's urging. He grew up in Boston, Massachusetts and earned his bachelor's degree from Harvard University.

Between college and law school, Redstone served in the United States Army during World War II as a code breaker. After his service to our country, he initially attended Georgetown University School of Law, but later went home and graduated from Harvard Law School in 1947. After his graduation from law school, Redstone was a Special Assistant to United States Attorney Thomas Clark (who later became an associate Justice of the United States Supreme Court). He then moved on to the Tax Division of the Department of Justice, practicing in both Washington, D.C. and San Francisco, California. After his time with the Department of Justice, Redstone spent several years in private practice.

In 1954, after seven years of practicing law, Redstone joined his father in the family business called Northeast Theater Corporation (the predecessor to National Amusements), which served as a holding company for theater, entertainment, and amusement assets. Redstone worked alongside his father for thirteen years before becoming CEO of National Amusements, as the company was then known.

Redstone is believed to have coined the phrase "content is king," based on his prescient belief that real money was to be made in production and ownership of content as opposed to merely distribution. While executing his vision to own content, Redstone went on a decade long buying spree that included the acquisition of such movie development companies as Columbia Pictures, Orion, 20th Century Fox, and Paramount Pictures.

In the late 1980s, after slowly acquiring stock in the company as an investment, Redstone launched a hostile takeover of Viacom, no doubt eying the premium content it controlled through properties such as Showtime, The Movie Channel, and MTV, which Viacom itself had acquired in 1985 from Warner Communications for $550 million. After adding Viacom to the National Amusements portfolio, Redstone continued to piece together high-quality assets in the entertainment industry. Having had the vision to see that "content is king," Redstone relied on his tenacity and determination to execute his business plan over many, many years. Indeed, Redstone, who is currently in his mid-nineties, is still involved in the business as Chairman emeritus (albeit not without controversy).

In his autobiography, *A Passion to Win*, Redstone describes having a "love affair" with his business. He further described the process of painstakingly cobbling together book, movie, and music content producers as "exhilarating," and one that clearly gave him energy rather than draining it from him. This does not mean that the process was always stress free, but rather Redstone could handle the stress because of the absolute love he had for what he was doing. He was executing a vision that came to him in his early days learning at his father's side.

Redstone's legal training and experience with tax law have served him well over his illustrious career. Yet it seems that the seeds of entrepreneurship were planted by his father during Sumner's childhood, and young Sumner seemed destined to make his mark in the business world rather than as a practicing lawyer.

RILEY BECHTEL—BECHTEL CORPORATION

Unlike Sumner Redstone, Riley Bechtel is probably not a recognizable name to most readers. Yet he is a multi-billionaire, and was the fourth-generation Chairman and Chief Executive Officer of Bechtel Corporation, a construction and engineering firm based in San Francisco, California. Bechtel's son, Brendan, is now the fifth-generation leader of this highly successful family enterprise that has been in business since 1898.

Riley Bechtel was born in Alameda County, California, in 1952. By 1966, Bechtel was spending his summers working in the family business, where he held various responsibilities, including the difficult task of field construction. He then attended the University of California (Davis), where he earned his Bachelor of Science in political science and psychology. He later earned his JD/MBA from Stanford University in 1977 and thereafter was admitted to practice law in the State of California.

Bechtel practiced law for four years with the firm Thelen, Marrin, Johnson & Bridges, where he performed corporate and commercial work for Bechtel Corp, among other clients. As with Redstone, while Bechtel was perhaps destined to return to the family business, he spent several important years learning the ropes as a business lawyer.

Bechtel eventually escaped the practice of law and rejoined the family business in 1981, where he started as a contract coordinator and piping superintendent. Here was a young, Stanford-educated lawyer who left the practice of law and went out into the field to learn his family's business from the ground up. Indeed, after six years spent paying his dues, Bechtel was named an executive vice president with the company. He learned the business as anyone from the outside would—by serving in different departments domestically and internationally. In the process, he earned the respect of his colleagues. In 1989, Bechtel was named president and chief operating officer of the company, and would later become chairman and chief executive officer.

Bechtel has since stepped down as chairman and chief executive officer of Bechtel Corporation due to his battle with Parkinson's disease. Nevertheless, he continues to serve as a member of the board of directors, and no doubt provides support to the company's current chief executive, his son Brendan.

Riley Bechtel was born into a situation that is foreign to most of us. His father represented the third generation of Bechtel men to lead Bechtel Corporation, and it is fair to say that Riley started with a leg up in life. Yet it seems that Bechtel's parents worked hard to avoid the perception (or reality) that their children would get things they had not earned simply because of the name on their birth certificate. Instead, Bechtel literally worked his way up from the bottom rung of the corporate ladder, starting in the field during his high school summers and ending up as chairman of the board. It was this diversity of experience, which included his (albeit brief) legal experience, that provided the foundation for Bechtel's remarkable success in growing the family business during his period of leadership. In the process, he made himself a billionaire.

STEPHEN RALES—DANAHER CORPORATION

Danaher Corporation is another highly successful "family business," that was founded by brothers Mitchell and Stephen Rales. Stephen Rales, a lawyer, was one of four sons of Ruth and Norman Rales. Norman, who was raised in an orphanage after losing his entire family in the Holocaust, pulled himself up by his bootstraps to become an entrepreneur in the building supply industry, a real estate investor, and later a noted philanthropist.

Stephen Rales seems to possess nearly all the Alpha Characteristics. He was born into a tightly-knit Jewish family, with a father who was a gritty entrepreneur and almost certainly instilled in his children (either directly or indirectly) a healthy appetite for risk. While his parents almost certainly could have given their boys a life of luxury, they instead instilled in their sons the values of discipline and of building a strong work ethic.

Stephen Rales was born in Maryland in 1951. He attended DePauw University, where he earned his Bachelor of Arts in 1973. After spending a few years learning the real estate business from his empire-building father, Rales attended American University, where he earned his JD in 1978.

Unlike Redstone and Bechtel, it does not appear that Rales ever formally practiced law outside of his own business. After about a year working in his father's real estate business, Rales left to form Equity Group Holdings, the predecessor to Danaher, with an initial focus on the adjacent business of mortgage loans. The Rales brothers pivoted quickly and used high-yield debt to acquire a variety of unsexy businesses, and then leveraged their unique operational approach to turn the businesses around and operate or sell them at a handsome profit. Within the first two years of founding the company, Danaher Corporation had acquired twelve different companies in a variety of industries.

Rales's legal education no doubt came in handy when Danaher pursued multiple hostile takeovers and was involved in a variety of legal disputes, one of which has become a seminal case in the canon of Delaware corporate law (*Rales v. Blasband*). His tight-knit, entrepreneurial family served as a support system and foundation that encouraged Rales to take risks, make his own way, and exercise the freedom to create a life of his own design. While Rales attended the well-respected universities of DePauw and American, he does not have the Ivy League or Stanford pedigree of Redstone and Bechtel. Clearly, such a pedigree is not necessary to earn massive success in business, as Stephen Rales's fortune is estimated to be at more than $4 billion.

Importantly, Stephen Rales adopted the generosity of his parents, is an active philanthropist, a patron of the arts, and acquired diverse experience through both his education and his participation in his father's businesses. This provided a solid foundation when he finally branched out with his brother Mitchell to start the company that would eventually become Danaher. Rales has led Danaher through a sustained period of exponential growth over the years, and his steady progress is a perfect example of one of the key Alpha Characteristics of "playing the long game." It appears to be by design that the company flies under the radar, as Rales has quietly built an empire comprised of many sleepy, yet wildly profitable, businesses.

HENRY SILVERMAN—CENDANT CORPORATION

Henry Silverman was born in 1940 into a Jewish family in Brooklyn, New York. Silverman lived a classic upper-middle-class New York childhood, thanks to his father's role as chief executive officer of commercial finance for James Talcott, Inc. As with other Alphas, Silverman served his country, in Henry's case as a member of the United States Naval Reserve during the Vietnam War.

Silverman graduated from Williams College in 1961 and earned his law degree from the University of Pennsylvania in 1964. Henry Silverman's escape from the practice of law represents perhaps the most circuitous path of any Alpha profiled in this book. Through that journey, Silverman gained a diverse set of experiences that served him extremely well in business.

Silverman was trained as a tax lawyer and spent several years in private practice. Frustrated by the restrictions placed on lawyers with respect to the freedom to advertise one's services, Silverman quickly realized that the constraints inherent in the practice of law were not for him. After deciding to escape law for the world of business, he took a position as an assistant to the highly successful entrepreneur and founder of Warner Communications, Steve Ross (not the same Stephen Ross who is profiled later in this book). Nevertheless, because his father had helped him obtain that job, Silverman decided to leave the position after a short tenure in order to pursue business opportunities of his own design.

Again, as with most (if not all) Alphas, Silverman had a deeply inherent independent streak, and he was determined to make his own way. Silverman's next step in his escape plan led him to investment banking. He went to work with White, Weld & Company, where he learned how to put deals together and, more importantly, get them closed.

While he learned a great deal through his training and practice as a lawyer, and then through his experience as a dealmaker, Silverman itched to be the shot-caller. Therefore, he pursued a series of entrepreneurial endeavors from the mid-1960s through the 1970s, but by most accounts, did not achieve world-class results. After almost twenty years building experience on his own, in 1984, Silverman joined Reliance Group Holdings, where he continued his development at the shoulder of corporate raider Saul Steinberg.

Drawing on his extremely diverse experience, Silverman led the acquisition by Reliance Group of the Days Inn franchise, and was reported to have earned a profit of $125 million upon its sale. From 1984 through 1991, Silverman went on another burst of learning, gaining diverse experience through a variety of opportunities. For example, Silverman spent six of those seven years as the chief executive officer of Telemundo before leaving to join the private equity behemoth The Blackstone Group in 1991.

Unfortunately, Silverman's tenure with Blackstone was cut short due to litigation by Prudential Insurance Company. An investment that Prudential made in a Reliance Group deal had gone bad, and had occurred on Silverman's watch, leading Prudential (a major Blackstone investor) to sue. Demonstrating his ability to overcome adversity, Silverman and Blackstone cleverly arranged for Silverman to become the chief executive officer of Hospitality Franchise Systems (HFS) in 1991, which was a Blackstone portfolio company. In that role, Silverman executed a brilliant period of growth. He transformed HFS into a company called Cendant, and then grew Cendant into a multi-billion-dollar diversified conglomerate with multiple hotel chain franchises, including the Ramada and Howard Johnson's brands.

While Silverman's escape from the practice of law was not linear or flawless, it was a path of his own design. He was opportunistic and willing to take on significant risk at various points during his business journey. In doing so, has amassed a fortune estimated to be more than $300 million. Henry Silverman's life is a tremendous example of the grit and determination it takes to make the jump from the practice of law to eventually running a multi-billion-dollar conglomerate. While Silverman's business life has been marked with periods of significant adversity, he exemplifies the importance of always moving forward and turning one's obstacles into a path to success.

MICHAEL JAHARIS—KOS PHARMACEUTICALS

Mike Jaharis was born in Evanston, Illinois in 1928 to Michael and Katerina Jaharis, who immigrated to the United States from the island of Lesvos in Greece. Mike served in the United States Army during the Korean War, where he managed logistics associated with the delivery of medical and pharmaceutical supplies.

After the war, Jaharis took an entry level pharmaceutical sales job with Miles Laboratories. As with many returning veterans, Jaharis sought additional educational opportunities and pursued his law degree at night from DePaul University. After earning his degree, Jaharis worked his way up in the Miles organization and eventually became a vice president and executive legal counsel. There, he focused on food and drug law and led the company's marketing efforts.

Jaharis spent more than ten years at Miles Laboratories and gained valuable experience in the process. Then, in 1972, a medical doctor and businessman from Philadelphia named Philip Frost convinced Jaharis to leave Miles and join him in the acquisition of a company called Key Pharmaceuticals. Jaharis had grown tired of the bureaucracy of the larger Miles organization, and yearned for an opportunity to build his own company. Willing to take the risk, Frost and Jaharis acquired Key Pharma in a stock-for-stock transaction (i.e., no cash).

The Key Pharma opportunity was a pure turnaround play. At the time of the acquisition, Key Pharma, a company focused on selling cold and flu remedies, was nearly insolvent. Under Jaharis's leadership, however, the company pursued new products and eventually developed an industry-leading asthma remedy, as well as a cardiovascular product. After growing the company for nearly fourteen years, Jaharis and Frost sold Key Pharma to Schering Plough for just under $1 billion. The transaction made both Jaharis and Frost very wealthy men.

As with many successful entrepreneurs, however, Jaharis was not done. Two years after the sale of Key Pharmaceuticals, Jaharis founded Kos Pharmaceuticals, which pioneered innovative therapies to treat cardiovascular disease. This time, Jaharis spent nearly eighteen years growing the business, which he eventually sold to Abbott Laboratories in 2006 for nearly $4 billion. Before his death in 2016, Jaharis remained active in business, making private investments in other companies in the pharmaceutical industry. As with many Alphas, Jaharis was a devoted family man and was very active in philanthropy and the arts.

Mike Jaharis is another Alpha who reached the pinnacle of success in his chosen field by drawing on his deeply ingrained Alpha Characteristics. He was raised in an immigrant family, where the values of hard work, generosity, and service were instilled in him from a young age. He was called to serve his country and, upon his return, set out to make his way in the world. He was willing to play the long game and grew comfortable accepting significant risk along the way.

Jaharis leveraged his legal training to rise through the ranks at Miles Laboratories, which enabled him to move from sales, to legal, to marketing, and eventually to the role of chief executive officer. The diversity of that experience no doubt gave him the courage to risk joining Frost and acquiring an insolvent pharmaceutical company with the goal of transforming it into a successful company of his own. Not only did he find success with Key Pharma, but he built multiple companies that created jobs and products that had a positive impact on millions of lives.

RANDALL J. KIRK—NEW RIVER PHARMACEUTICALS

Randall J. ("RJ") Kirk has described himself as a lifelong student of business, and has perhaps one of the most unique stories that took him from a small town in Virginia to the top of the pharmaceutical industry. Kirk was born in California in 1954, the son of an Air Force officer. As with many military families, the Kirks moved around quite a bit, eventually settling in Virginia. After graduating from high school in the early 1970s, Kirk took a job selling cars and motorcycles while simultaneously taking classes at nearby Radford College.

Kirk graduated from Radford in 1976 and decided to pursue a legal education because he thought it would give him a foundation upon which he could pursue a variety of endeavors. He graduated from the University of Virginia in 1979 and was admitted to the Bar of the Commonwealth of Virginia in 1980.

Kirk practiced law for eleven years in the small town of Bland County, Virginia, where he was the town's only lawyer. As such, Kirk's general practice resulted in him gaining experience in a variety of legal matters. While he was growing his practice, he also started to dabble in investments outside of law, including in a UHF television station.

In 1983, Kirk's interest in seeking business experience outside of the practice of law eventually led him to partner with a local pharmacist to found a next-day pharmaceutical distributor called General Injectables and Vaccines. By 1990, after eleven years as a lawyer, Kirk stepped away from his law practice to focus exclusively on growing General Injectables. The move proved to be brilliant, as Kirk and his partner sold General Injectables in 1998 to Henry Schein, Inc. for $145 million. While this was a nice win for the small-town Virginia lawyer, he was just getting started.

Two years before Kirk sold General Injectables, he formed a new company called New River Pharmaceuticals, which was focused on developing innovative drug therapies. Only six years later, in 2004, Kirk led New River through an IPO, which would enable the company to fuel its continued, rapid growth. In 2006, Shire Pharmaceuticals acquired New River for $2.6 billion, which, in addition to being a fantastic outcome for all shareholders, made RJ Kirk a billionaire.

As with Mike Jaharis, RJ Kirk wasn't content to merely ride off into the sunset after his initial success. Rather, his passion for business has led him to make highly strategic investments in other life sciences and biotech companies, several of which have had multi-billion dollar exits of their own. In addition, as with many Alphas, Kirk is active with his family, political causes, and philanthropy.

RJ Kirk's story is an ideal example of the benefit of playing the long game. He was a small-town, general practice lawyer for more than ten years, and he used his practice to generate the income necessary to fund his lifestyle while also (more importantly) providing the springboard that allowed him to branch out into business. His escape was not immediate; rather, he planted seeds, some of which never really sprouted (such as the investment in the UHF television station), and others (the investment in General Injectables) that provided the means of escape from the practice of law. He exhibited a healthy appetite for risk by leaving the "sure thing" of his well-established law practice (where he was essentially the only game in town) for the rough-and-tumble world of the pharmaceutical business. After his first taste of success, when many would have taken their chips and walked away, he has passionately continued his mission to improve the world through life sciences and biotechnology. The clear lesson to be learned from RJ Kirk is that properly focused, a lawyer who has the desire to pursue success in business, is willing to put in the time, and is willing to play the long game can achieve remarkable things outside of the practice of law.

ROBERT ROWLING—TRT HOLDINGS, INC.

Like Riley Bechtel, Bob Rowling is an example of one who had the benefit of an extremely wealthy family backing him up, but nevertheless was committed to making his own mark on the business world. Rowling was born in Corpus Christi, Texas in 1953. His father, Reese Rowling, was a geologist who (along with a partner) founded a company called Tana Oil and Gas, which they later sold to Texaco in 1989 for nearly $500 million.

After earning his undergraduate degree from the University of Texas and his law degree from Southern Methodist University, Bob Rowling practiced tax law for one year before leaving in 1981 to help his father grow Tana. After the sale of Tana to Texaco, the younger Rowling decided to use his share of the proceeds to venture into a new industry. By 1990, the hotel business was in recession, and Bob identified that industry as one that offered some significant bargains—and thus the opportunity for meaningful returns. While his father was skeptical (he told Bob that he would most likely "lose his shirt"), he supported Bob in his new venture. Over the next four years, TRT Holdings acquired eight properties totaling about $150 million in invested capital. However, the assets themselves were worth far more, and Rowling and his team settled in intent on learning the hotel business.

By 1996, with several years of experience under his belt, Rowling leaped at the opportunity to expand into the higher-end of the hotel world with the acquisition of the then-struggling Omni hotel chain for approximately $500 million. TRT has since expanded the Omni franchise to include more than sixty hotels. In addition to these impressive assets, the company also owns the Gold's Gym franchise and has made other opportunistic investments.

It cannot be denied that Bob Rowling had a significant advantage by being able to leave the practice of law after only one year to join his father's already-valuable oil and gas company. Nevertheless, while he could have coasted through life as the wealthy heir of a successful entrepreneur, Bob Rowling chose the path that most Alphas choose—playing the hand they're dealt and seeking to improve upon it. Indeed, Bob has turned what was already significant wealth following the sale of Tana into a fortune (his net worth is estimated to be more than $5 billion), has built tremendous value in multiple industries, and has provided jobs and avenues to wealth creation for countless others along the way.

CHARLIE MUNGER—BERKSHIRE HATHAWAY

While perhaps not as famous as his partner, Warren Buffett, Charlie Munger is an Alpha who exemplifies the value of diligence and seizing opportunity. Munger was born in Omaha, Nebraska. During his youth, he briefly worked for Buffett & Sons Grocery Store, which was run by Warren Buffett's family, although he did not meet his future partner until many years later. Munger left Nebraska for the University of Michigan, but shortly thereafter joined the United States Army Air Corps as a Second Lieutenant during World War II. He studied meteorology during his service by attending California Institute of Technology, and then continued his military service in Alaska.

Following his military service, even though he did not have an undergraduate degree, Munger moved to Boston, was admitted to Harvard

Law School, and graduated magna cum laude in 1949. Following graduation, Munger picked up his family and moved west, accepting a position with the firm Wright & Garrett (which later became Musick, Peeler & Garrett).

During the first six years growing his practice in Los Angeles, Munger overcame crushing personal adversity. In 1953, at twenty-nine years old, he was divorced from his first wife, whom he had married when he was just twenty-one. Munger lost nearly all his material possessions in the divorce, and shortly after learned that his young son, Teddy, had leukemia. Munger struggled to rebuild his personal and professional lives while caring for his terminally ill son at the same time. In 1955, Teddy Munger died at the age of nine.

Despite this immense personal tragedy, Munger somehow soldiered on and focused on delivering value in the world, both personally and professionally. In 1956, he married Nancy Barry, with whom he would have four children. (Each of them also had two children from previous marriages.) Together, Charlie and Nancy built a beautiful personal life, while professionally Munger continued to build his law practice at what was then the firm Musick, Peeler & Garrett.

In 1959, Munger made a connection that would change his life forever. While attending a dinner party back in Omaha, Nebraska, Munger met a man named Warren Buffett, and the two immediately hit it off. They started to share investment ideas, and Buffett eventually became one of Munger's law firm clients. Just as this relationship started to blossom, Munger and some of his colleagues itched to run and break out on their own.

In 1962, the law firm Munger, Tolles & Hills (which would eventually become Munger, Tolles & Olson) was launched by the three named partners, along with two younger attorneys from Musick, Peeler. Munger focused his practice in real estate law, but increasingly spent more time managing his personal investments on the side. As with many Alphas, Munger kept a foot in the legal world until he was sure he could make a real go of private investment management outside of it.

Charlie Munger finally executed his escape from the practice of law in 1965, relenting to the urging of his friend Mr. Buffett, who believed Munger was more suited for the role of principal than agent. Interestingly, he and Buffett would not formally join forces for another thirteen years.

During that intervening time, Munger experienced the highs and lows that come with entrepreneurship. He dabbled with real estate development and ran what today would be considered a hedge fund—an investment partnership that traded public securities. While Munger's investment partnership generated compounded annual returns of almost 20 percent between 1962 and 1975, he decided to shutter the firm in 1976. No doubt, this decision was colored by weathering two extremely difficult years in 1973 (losses of 32 percent) and 1974 (losses of 31 percent). Again, Munger looked adversity square in the eye and continued on, in large part because he was always playing the long game.

The rest of Munger's story is the stuff of legend. He and Warren Buffett eventually partnered together and have built one of the most impressive businesses in American history. Buffett credits Munger with convincing him of the virtues of buying high-quality assets, even those that may trade at a premium to certain competitors, and then building the value of those assets over the long term. It's hard to argue with this strategy, which has produced massive returns for Berkshire Hathaway investors, and has made both Munger and Buffett billionaires in the process.

Charlie Munger's story is perhaps one of the most encouraging for those who are currently practicing law, but looking for a way to branch out from the traditional path. Munger not only practiced law for sixteen years, but in the process founded his own law firm and made a key connection at a dinner party that became the launch pad for his future success. It is important to note, however, that Munger did not meet Buffett and seek to turn that connection into immediate personal gain. Rather, Munger and Buffett had a genuine, personal connection. Neither of them sought anything from the other, except for sincere friendship and an exchange of ideas. As their relationship developed, Munger delivered value first (i.e., sharing his investment ideas with his friend), and then later earned Buffett's business and, with it, an opportunity to showcase his talents. In doing so, Munger not only impressed Buffett with his legal skill, but also demonstrated his value outside the practice of law.

By playing the long game, Munger branched out on his own well before he and Buffett finally partnered up, and the law firm that Munger started with a few partners and associates is still in existence today. It is considered one of the top firms in the United States and still bears Munger's name on the masthead.

The lesson of Charlie Munger's success is not "hope to meet someone like Warren Buffett and see if you can join him." Rather, it is that those who choose to make an escape from law may have to practice for many years before they can do so, and should be thoughtful about their pursuit of opportunities as they branch out. In other words, character traits like patience, persistence, seeking to deliver value first, and lifelong commitment to learning will pay off in the end—but one cannot expect earn massive success overnight.

JOHN ANDERSON—TOPA EQUITIES LTD.

John Anderson exemplifies the value of leveraging all of one's Alpha Characteristics to achieve success both in and out of the practice of law. Anderson was born in Minneapolis, Minnesota in 1917. His father was a barber, and Anderson's first entrepreneurial endeavor was selling popcorn to passersby outside his father's barber shop. The strong work ethic instilled in Anderson during his early years led to impressive academic success. Anderson was valedictorian of his high school class and earned his B.A. in Economics from UCLA in 1940, where he was a stand-out member of the ice hockey team.

After college, Anderson went to Harvard Business School, where he earned his MBA just as World War II erupted. As with many of his generation, Anderson answered his nation's call and joined the Navy. He served as an aide to an admiral and studied for the CPA exam at the same time, passing the exam upon his return to the states. After the war, Anderson worked for the accounting firm Arthur Anderson during the day and attended law school at night, eventually earning his law degree from Loyola Law School in 1950. Anderson was first in his class at Loyola and accepted a teaching position upon graduation.

With Anderson's entrepreneurial background and diverse experience through his military service, teaching, and work as an accountant, it is not surprising that he started his own law firm (known as Kindel & Anderson) just three years out of law school. It was not until 1956, as he was approaching forty years old, that Anderson pursued his first entrepreneurial endeavor outside his legal practice.

Anderson had developed a niche representing beverage companies on matters of licensing and distribution. Through his expertise in that niche, a client approached him seeking assistance to find a buyer for its business. After taking a look, Anderson decided to make a bid on his own. In the process, he founded Ace Beverage Company, and through that vehicle acquired the exclusive rights to distribute Budweiser beer in the Los Angeles market. This move served as the foundation for what has become a diversified, family-owned business with interests in a variety of industries.

In 1980, when Anderson was sixty-three years old, he founded Topa Properties, Ltd., which acquired real estate in California, Hawaii, and the US Virgin Islands. Today, Topa Properties owns more than four million square feet of commercial space and more than 4,500 residential units, and Topa and its subsidiaries have also ventured into automobile dealerships, agriculture, insurance, and various other industries.

As with many Alphas profiled in these pages, Anderson brought diverse and valuable experience to the practice of law, and then later into his other entrepreneurial endeavors. He served under an Admiral in the Navy, spent time as a practicing accountant, and performed so well in law school that he spent several years teaching law while building his legal practice. As with many of those Alphas who spent more than a year or two practicing, Anderson took the entrepreneurial step of forming his own law firm. Yet, as he gained experience by representing the interests of his business clients, he was drawn to take a seat at the other side of the table. When opportunity presented itself through the acquisition of the exclusive Budweiser distribution rights, Anderson leveraged all his experience up to that point to make the deal—*his* deal—happen. Moreover, he was in his mid-thirties when he started his own law firm, almost forty years old when he made his first move outside the practice of law, and more than sixty years old when he started to diversify his holdings and branch out into new industries. Anderson's example, along with many others you will find in this book, puts to rest the excuse that one is ever "too old" or too far along in the practice of law to become an entrepreneur. In fact, one could argue, that the more experience one has, the more likely they will be successful in their entrepreneurial endeavors.

GERALD J. FORD—BANKING

Jerry Ford (not to be confused with the former president, Gerald R. Ford) grew up in Pampa, Texas, the son of an auto mechanic and a schoolteacher. As a teenager, Ford worked alongside his father in the family auto-body shop and worked on a nearby farm in the summers. Ford yearned for a bigger life outside of his small town and eyed entrepreneurship as his ticket to personal freedom. While he wasn't quite sure how he would do it, he believed that earning a degree would help him get there.

Ford earned his B.A. in 1966 and his JD in 1969, both from Southern Methodist University. When asked why he attended law school, Ford noted that the people who seemed to be most successful in Pampa were the lawyers. He thought that earning a law degree might help him pursue his goal of maximum personal freedom. Indeed, Ford would leverage his legal education as his gateway to massive success in business.

Following his graduation from law school, Ford worked for several years in the real estate industry, serving as general counsel to several closely held family companies. In 1975, at the age of thirty-one, Ford decided to make his escape from the traditional path inside the practice of law and, with two partners, scraped together $1.2 million to buy a controlling interest in the small, regional First National Bank of Post, Texas. He later sold the bank at an impressive profit. This was the beginning of a run that has lasted more than forty years and has resulted in buying, repositioning, and exiting troubled banks, producing significant gains for Ford, his partners, and his investors.

While Ford's success has primarily been in the world of banking, one could reasonably conclude that he would have been equally successful in a variety of industries. At his core, Ford is an entrepreneur, a dealmaker, and a master operator. He was raised in a middle-class family in a small town in Texas, and did not start his career with a sterling pedigree or powerful connections. Rather, his motivation can be traced back to his early experiences working in his father's auto body shop, which planted the seed of desire for future success in business. Jerry Ford exemplifies the value that can be derived from the Alpha Characteristics that many of us share—working class roots, an entrepreneurial background (either through our family members or on our own), a healthy appetite for risk, and an ability to overcome adversity and play the long game (Ford not only survived during the savings and loan and banking crisis that hit Texas hard in the 1980s, but was actually perfectly positioned to extend his holdings during that difficult period.)

* * *

In this chapter, we have focused on ten men who successfully transitioned out of the practice of law and into directly operating companies in a variety of industries, ranging from entertainment to banking, and a lot in between. In many cases, these men have built enterprises that own interests in many companies, each of which employ hundreds, if not thousands of people.

While each of these individuals pursued business and industry in slightly different ways, they share many common Alpha Characteristics that helped them achieve massive success. Several of these individuals served in the military in some capacity. Moreover, while several of these men attended Ivy League institutions, others (Stephen Rales, RJ Kirk, and Jerry Ford, for example) stayed close to home and earned their respective educations at other, well-regarded, universities. Each of the men profiled in this chapter had strong family bonds. In many cases, their entrepreneurial roots can be traced back to experiences with their fathers or other family members. Many of these men overcame significant adversity (both personal and professional) on their way to success in business, and each of them developed a healthy appetite for risk. Finally, each of these men exemplifies the value and importance of playing the long game, and other than Mike Jaharis (who died in 2016 at the age of eighty-seven) and John Anderson (who died in 2011 at the age of ninety-three), each remains actively involved in their businesses to this day.

This last point warrants additional emphasis. My hope is that the readers of this book will range in age from early twenties (those considering or currently attending law school) to late forties, early fifties, or older (those currently practicing law and considering an escape into entrepreneurship). Each of the Alphas in this chapter practiced law in some form, with a few who practiced for more than ten years before they made their escape. But, none of the Alphas in this chapter sought (or achieved) overnight success. In several cases, these men traded the safety and security provided by their respective law practices, for the uncertainty of business. They no doubt raised some eyebrows among their partners and peers, and some had to take a step back financially before they reaped the rewards of their business endeavors. Nevertheless, each of these men perfectly illustrate the point that if one seeks to add value in the marketplace and earn maximum personal freedom in the process, the financial rewards will come in some form if one is merely willing to play the long game.

CHAPTER FOUR

Empire Builders

One of the most common transitions from law into business is the move from law to real estate development and investment. It is common in part because real estate transactions involve significant legal issues, as property rights are at the core of the American experience, and because transactional lawyers are often called on to help real estate investors, developers, and managers structure and finance large-scale projects.

In this chapter, we examine the transitions of five former lawyers who escaped the practice of law and achieved Alpha status by methodically building diverse real estate empires. As with all the Alphas profiled in this book, these men leveraged their legal training along with their individual Alpha Characteristics to successfully make the escape from the practice of law. As you will see, while these individuals chose to make their escape through real estate, they likely would have been successful in any field. In each case, these men are entrepreneurs who just happened to find significant opportunities with "bricks and sticks" as opposed to other businesses. More importantly, each profile in this chapter demonstrates that those who can tolerate risk and leverage their legal expertise in support of their efforts in almost any business enterprise can not only successfully escape the practice of law, but can also drive immense value in the marketplace.

SAM ZELL—EQUITY GROUP INVESTMENTS

Sam Zell is one of my business heroes. (The others, Reggie Lewis and Teddy Forstmann, are both profiled in Chapter Five.) Zell has had exceptional business success, ventured into many different arenas, is generous in support of causes and organizations close to his heart, and is refreshingly genuine and direct. But his story, while remarkable, began just like many of ours.

Zell was born and raised in Highland Park, Illinois to Jewish immigrant parents. His father, a former grain trader turned jewelry broker turned real estate investor, instilled entrepreneurial lessons in Sam from an early age. When Sam was an undergrad at the University of Michigan, he aligned himself with a local real estate entrepreneur and negotiated his way into a gig managing the entrepreneur's fifteen-unit apartment building in Ann Arbor in exchange for room and board. Eventually, Zell enlisted the services of his fraternity brother Robert H. Lurie, and the men embarked on an impressive run as the owner/managers of multiple apartment units throughout the Ann Arbor area. By the time Zell graduated from law school at the University of Michigan, he and Lurie were managing more than 4,000 units and owned nearly 200 units on their own.

As his graduation from law school approached, Sam decided that he had to test himself outside the small-town confines of Ann Arbor. Therefore, he sold off his interest in the apartment business to Lurie and set out to begin his professional career in his hometown of Chicago. Zell had not pursued his legal studies with visions of spending the rest of his career in the practice of law. Rather, he saw formal legal study as a vehicle to develop expertise in deal-making, which he believed was his unique gift. Still, he attempted to find a position with a law firm in order to gain experience. After being rejected forty-three times (ostensibly because his impressive success in business was a red flag to potential law firm employers that he wouldn't stick around for long), he accepted a position with the Chicago law firm of Yates & Holleb. Not surprisingly, he lasted one week.

Remarkably, when Zell told the partner with whom he worked that he was leaving the firm to pursue deals on his own, the partner expressed admiration for Zell's guts, offered to invest alongside him, and allowed him to continue to work out of the firm's office. As a twenty-five-year-old man fresh out of law school, Zell drove a significant amount of business to the law firm and was initially paid half of the fees generated by the clients he referred. He was so successful, however, that the firm eventually reduced his share down to 25 percent. Even after reducing his referral fees, within the span of a year, Zell was earning more from his share of the fees than some junior partners at the firm were taking home. He was doing all this while focusing the bulk of his efforts on building his real estate business.

After eighteen months at Yates & Holleb, Zell felt he was still living under someone else's rules. He left the firm for good and went into the real estate business fulltime, setting up shop in a spare office in his brother-in-law Roger's law office. Soon, however, the complexities of running a rapidly growing real estate firm frustrated Zell, who preferred selling and making deals to administrative minutia. So he reunited with his former partner Bob Lurie, who had a penchant for the back-office details. That partnership, which began in 1968, would last the next twenty years. Following Lurie's death in 1990, Zell continued to build public and private real estate partnerships, all the while staying true to his model of buying undervalued assets, improving (or "repositioning") them, and then selling them at a profit. Perhaps the greatest example of his intuitive feel for the market was his 2007 sale of Equity Office Properties Trust to Blackstone Group for $39 billion, shortly before the real estate market took a big hit. While this deal would also turn out to be a good one for Blackstone, Zell's knack for deal-making made him a billionaire many times over.

Zell is still an active entrepreneur. At various stages of his career, he has been involved in the energy, transportation, media, and sports industries, with varying degrees of success. In addition, Zell has used his wealth to support charitable causes and the arts. He has inspired future entrepreneurs through the Zell/Lurie Real Estate Center at Wharton and the Zell-Lurie Institute for Entrepreneurship at the University of Michigan. Zell has said that, while he found law school boring and absolutely hated the brief time he spent practicing law, his legal education provided him a distinct advantage in building his business, as it taught him how to analyze, think, and assess risk.

RICHARD LEFRAK—LEFRAK ORGANIZATION

Richard Lefrak is a real estate entrepreneur who took an existing family enterprise and leveraged his legal background and other experiences to transform the company into the largest landlord in New York. Lefrak was born in New York in 1945 into a very entrepreneurial family. His grandfather, Harry, was an immigrant who got his start working in the trades, and eventually worked his way up to become a subcontractor on larger development projects. Through pure grit and determination, Harry Lefrak started to cobble together development deals with a few partners and from there, steadily built the family's real estate holdings.

Richard Lefrak's father, Sam, represented the second generation of the Lefrak Organization, and led the company through a period of explosive growth, adding units and extending the family's reach across the city. Sam involved Richard in the business from a very young age, as he would take him to the office on weekends and on walkthroughs on the company's various projects. Richard worked in the business throughout high school until he left for Amherst College, where he earned his undergraduate degree in 1967.

Sam wanted Richard to join the business immediately following his graduation from college, but a reluctant Richard opted instead to pursue his law degree. He attended Columbia University and earned his JD in 1970. Upon graduation from law school, Richard was thrust into the family business, and was immediately given responsibility for a new development project in New Jersey. The project was ultimately very successful, and remains part of the company's residential portfolio today. It marked the beginning of a remarkable run in the real estate business for the Lefrak Organization.

Richard was elevated to president in 1975, and took over as CEO after his father's death in 2003. The father and son could not be more different in terms of their respective styles and approach to the business. Sam developed a reputation as a straight-shooter who was gruff and direct. By contrast, Richard is more cerebral and low key in his approach. But with each generation, the Lefrak men have demonstrated a unique ability to immerse themselves in every detail of the business. This has enabled them to consistently develop large scale real estate projects with tight control on budgets and costs, thus delivering tremendous profit. While each member of the Lefrak family has made a unique impact on the business, what has been consistent is their noble work ethic, conservative use of leverage, and a multigenerational perspective.

Richard's sons, Harrison and Jamie, are the fourth generation of Lefrak men to be directly involved in the business at a high level. Harrison (who is also a lawyer) leads the financial aspects of the business, and Jamie is involved on the residential and development side.

As we have seen with other Alphas who, to a certain extent, "inherit" a successful family enterprise, those who achieve the greatest success are grateful for the blessing of starting off with a valuable business, but adopt it as their personal mission to leave the business (and the family) better off than when they took over. Richard Lefrak answered that call and has delivered sizeable value through his family business. Moreover, he has leveraged his legal education in support of his efforts to grow the Lefrak Organization. He has encouraged his sons (the next generation to lead the family business) to pursue higher education, which will provide a deep well of knowledge from which the family can continue to draw as they face the challenges and adversity of managing and growing a real estate enterprise that has endured for more than 100 years.

NEIL BLUHM—JMB REALTY CORP

Neil Bluhm is a billionaire real estate and casino magnate who overcame significant adversity early in his life on his way to massive success in business. Bluhm was born in Chicago in 1938. His mother was a bookkeeper. Bluhm's father left the family when Neil was just thirteen years old, and so he was raised by his mother and grandparents.

While Bluhm's family may have lacked deep financial resources and material possessions, they blessed him with something arguably much more valuable—an iron work ethic and the belief that by applying that dedication to his chosen field, he could achieve great things in America, a land of fabulous opportunity. With that in mind, Bluhm worked his way into the University of Illinois, where he earned his undergraduate degree in 1959.

After earning his CPA, Bluhm attended Northwestern University and earned his law degree in 1962.

After graduating from law school, Bluhm joined the prestigious Chicago law firm Mayer, Brown & Platt, where he was a tax lawyer and earned partnership with the firm at the age of thirty-one. As he was building his practice, Bluhm remained close with Judd Malkin and Robert Judelson. The three men had developed strong bonds growing up together in the Rogers Park section of Chicago. Malkin (who had also earned his CPA after graduating from Illinois) initially followed his father's footsteps into the automobile business by running a Toyota dealership, but started to dabble in real estate with Judelson, who was a real estate broker and had also been Bluhm's roommate at Illinois.

Although Bluhm was relatively comfortable as a partner at Mayer Brown (certainly considering his humble beginnings), he was hungry to build something and earn the freedom that entrepreneurship can provide. Malkin and Judelson finally convinced their friend to join them, and Bluhm executed his escape from the practice of law in 1969. That year, Judelson, Malkin, and Bluhm formed JMB Realty, focused on pursuing real estate investment and development transactions.

Bluhm's background structuring transactions and providing advice concerning partnership and tax law proved invaluable to JMB. Bluhm brought certain credibility to the team that opened some crucial doors with investors during the early days. While, as JMB syndicated projects by raising equity on a deal-by-deal basis through limited partnerships, Bluhm's expertise allowed the company to design and sell creative structures and opportunities to its investors. The partners had a healthy appetite for risk, but they focused on high-quality properties, believing that during an economic downturn, the last properties to take a hit were the premier assets.

During the early days, the partners were not making loads of money, and each took significant risk in striking out together. For his part, Bluhm left behind the relative comfort, security, and prestige of life as a partner with a large, international law firm, and traded it for the uncertain life as a real estate entrepreneur. Bluhm told *Forbes* that during those early days, his "credit card was [his] net worth." While the partnership had a successful and profitable run over a nearly twenty-year period, they also suffered through a real estate crash during the early 1990s. Nevertheless, Bluhm demonstrated his grit and determination, emerging from those tough years by expanding into private equity, casino, and gaming investments.

Neil Bluhm was heavily influenced by his hardscrabble early days on the North Side of Chicago. His family instilled in him the values of hard work and determination, and supported him as he pursued his dream to achieve something bigger and better with his life. He built strong relationships with his childhood friends, which eventually provided his route of escape from the practice of law. Bluhm exhibited the Alpha Characteristic of a high tolerance for risk throughout his career. By accepting risk and taking a long-term view of his professional life, Neil Bluhm has become a billionaire, produced fantastic returns for his investors, and provided opportunities for countless people along the way.

THOMAS BARRACK—COLONY NORTHSTAR

The story of Thomas Barrack, the founder of Colony Capital, is a study in the value of preparing oneself with the skills necessary to add value in a variety of ways, and then being prepared to seize opportunity when it presents itself. Barrack was born in California, where his mother was a homemaker and his father ran the family grocery store. His grandparents immigrated to the United States from Lebanon, and Barrack inherited his work ethic and entrepreneurial spirit from his family.

Barrack's father worked eighteen-hour days in the family store, where a young Tom would stack the shelves and work the register after school. As Barrack said in an interview with *Fortune*, while he was never the smartest or most talented person, he was never afraid to take calculated risks, and he would simply outwork and outlast his competitors.

Barrack graduated from the University of Southern California in 1969, where he was a member of the National Championship Rugby team. He then pursued a law degree, earning his JD in 1972 from the University of San

Diego. Of all the Alphas profiled in this book, Barrack's path following law school may be the most colorful.

Barrack's first job as a lawyer was with the law firm Kalmbach, DeMarco, Knapp & Chillingworth, which had been founded by Herbert Kalmbach, President Richard Nixon's personal lawyer. Barrack, drawing on the work ethic he observed in members of his family, worked long hours, often arriving to the office as early as 5:00 a.m., even on weekends. One early morning, a partner at the law firm noticed that Barrack was already at his desk, working diligently. The partner invited Barrack to work on an important new transaction—a gas liquidation project in Saudi Arabia—for one of the firm's largest clients, Fluor Corporation.

Eventually, the firm needed someone to travel to Saudi Arabia to negotiate the deal. Barrack earned the opportunity to become the lead project finance lawyer on the transaction, negotiating with ARAMCO and the Kingdom of Saudi Arabia on behalf of Fluor. Through that transaction, Barrack developed relationships with some of the young Saudis who were also working on it, and those relationships led to new and exciting opportunities.

Barrack endured tough working conditions in Saudi Arabia (as noted in the *Fortune* magazine article, Barrack slept on a "filthy cot in a Riyadh dormitory without indoor plumbing"), yet realized that he was developing an invaluable skill—serving as an agent for wealthy Texas contractors in their business dealings with Saudi sheikhs. After closing the Fluor transaction, Barrack left the law firm and went to work evaluating transactions on behalf of two young Saudi princes he had met during that deal. Barrack also invested the time and effort to learn the Arabic language, as well as the cultural mores that were necessary to succeed in business in that country.

While he would have had no way of knowing it at the time, the experience he was gaining in Saudi Arabia would also make him extremely valuable to certain investors back in the United States. In 1976, just four years after he graduated from law school, Barrack was approached by Lonnie Dunn, a Texas based investor, to help him out of a jam related to an investment in Haiti. Barrack leveraged his relationship with the Saudi princes to orchestrate a deal between Dunn, the Haitian government, and the Saudis that resulted in a win-win-win (and "-win" for Barrack) all the way around.

Barrack impressed Dunn so much that Dunn coaxed him into returning to the United States to run a company that was focused on constructing industrial buildings and office parks in California. Although Dunn sold that company in 1980, Barrack stayed on for two years after the transaction to run the business for the new buyer. From there, he briefly worked in government (during the Reagan Administration) and as an investment banker for E.F. Hutton & Company. Then, in 1984 (at the age of thirty-seven), he was recruited by billionaire Robert Bass to again work on real estate deals.

For the next seven years, Barrack worked with Bass on many big, creative real estate transactions that added to Bass's already vast fortune and, in the process, made Barrack a very wealthy man. Following the path forged by all the Alphas profiled in this book, in 1991, Barrack finally made a move on his own and formed Colony Capital, a real estate private equity firm. Since then, Colony has invested in a variety of assets, including some highly lucrative distressed debt investments in the 1990s.

Thomas Barrack is a perfect example of what is possible if one with solid legal training and experience is open to delivering value first, without any expectation of reciprocation, and then seizes opportunity when it is presented. While Barrack may not have started his career with a sterling academic pedigree, deep rolodex, or vast amounts of family capital, he leveraged his work ethic, creativity, and willingness to sacrifice in the short term to open opportunities that would deliver massive returns in the long term. At each step along the way, Barrack worked to exceed expectations (of the partners in his law firm, the Saudi princes, Lonnie Dunn, and Robert Bass), trusting that if he delivered immense value, the rewards would surely follow. Today, Barrack is a billionaire and continues to manage an impressive portfolio of real estate and other private investments, all the while living the life of maximum personal freedom that comes with being a successful entrepreneur.

BERNARD F. SAUL, II—B.F. SAUL COMPANY
& SAUL CENTERS, INC.

Bernard Saul is one of the handful of Alphas who, despite being born into wealth, did not take his good fortune for granted but rather accepted the blessing of his birth and did his part to further the family legacy. Saul is the third-generation Chairman and CEO of Saul Centers, Inc., a family-owned real estate investment trust in the Washington, D.C. area that owns a multi-billion-dollar portfolio of shopping center, residential, and commercial properties in D.C., Maryland, and Virginia.

Saul is a very private person. In 1998, *Forbes* quoted him as saying, "If you forgot about me, I'd be grateful." A devout Catholic and supporter of many Catholic charities, Saul earned his undergraduate degree from Villanova University and his law degree from the University of Virginia in 1957. Although details are sparse, Saul joined the family business and proceeded to build upon this grandfather's legacy. B.F. Saul Company has a deep history in property management, leasing, development, insurance, and related real estate activities. The company also developed an expertise with mortgage financing very early in its history. While other mortgage lenders went bankrupt during the Crash of 1929 and the Great Depression that followed, B.F. Saul Company thrived.

It is therefore unsurprising that perhaps one of Bernard F. Saul, II's greatest accomplishments was leveraging the family's expertise in mortgage lending to found, scale and sell an immensely valuable financial institution. In 1969, Saul acquired an existing savings and loan charter and formed Chevy Chase Savings and Loan Association, which eventually became Chevy Chase Federal Savings Bank, and finally Chevy Chase Bank. At its peak, Chevy Chase Bank had more than 290 branches in three states and the District of Columbia, and had more than $14 billion in deposits. In addition, B.F. Saul & Company was the bank's mortgage subsidiary and was one of the largest mortgage originators in the region. Finally, in 2009 Saul led the sale of Chevy Chase Bank to Capital One for nearly $500 million.

While Saul's path from law school to the family business may have been preordained, one would have difficulty arguing that he has not made his own mark. Although he never practiced law directly, there can be little doubt that his legal education has served him well in the fields of real estate and finance. The Alpha Characteristics of strong familial connections, an entrepreneurial heritage, deep faith, and a vision that extends beyond his own lifetime have served Saul well as he's led the growth of B.F. Saul Company for the last fifty years.

CHAPTER FIVE

Allocators of Capital

As with the transition from law to real estate, the transition from the practice of law to the allocation of capital as an investor through vehicles such as venture capital, private equity, and leveraged buyouts is entirely logical, particularly for those lawyers who excel at analyzing and managing risk. Many transactional lawyers who routinely advise on financing and merger and acquisition transactions gain deep expertise in evaluating and structuring those deals and, thus, can bring creativity and discipline to the process.

In this chapter, we study ten men who escaped the practice of law and made some of the best investments in United States business history. Among this group are several individuals who are actually credited with creating the venture capital, private equity, and LBO investment industries. Also among them are two of my three business "mentors" profiled in this book: Reginald Lewis, who was the first African American to lead the buyout of a multinational, billion-dollar company, and Teddy Forstmann, who during his life experienced the highest highs and the lowest lows on his way to building one of the great buyout firms of the 1980s.

* * *

REGINALD LEWIS—TLC BEATRICE

The rise of Reginald Lewis from the inner city of Baltimore, Maryland to the pinnacle of high finance is perhaps the most remarkable profile you will read in this book. Reggie Lewis is the only African American on the Alpha list, and is also perhaps the best example of one who achieved success in both the practice of law *and* his chosen path in business. As noted earlier, Reggie Lewis is also one of my personal business heroes, one whom I most closely associate with and whose success I would like to emulate.

Reggie Lewis was born in Baltimore, Maryland on December 7, 1942. Lewis's father and mother divorced when he was young, but his mother remarried and Lewis was extremely close with his mother, stepfather, half-siblings, and grandparents on his mother's side. From a very young age, Lewis started working nights and weekends at the country club where his grandfather was maître de. Through that experience, Lewis learned to mix in different cultures, and his grandfather instilled in him a deep sense of pride and a belief that he could accomplish anything if he was willing to put in the work.

Lewis was a three-sport athlete in high school, and was recruited to play quarterback at Virginia State University, a historically black college. As a result of an injury, Lewis was unable to play football throughout his entire college career, but this turned out to be a blessing in disguise, as it allowed him to focus entirely on his studies. Although he initially struggled in college, Lewis eventually became a dean's list student at Virginia State. Thanks to his academic performance (and the assistance of a professor he had impressed), he earned an opportunity at Harvard University School of Law in a summer program supported by the Rockefeller Foundation. This program introduced exceptional students at historically black universities to legal studies prior to completing their undergraduate degrees. Lewis performed so well and made such a positive impression on certain faculty members at the law school that he became the only documented case of a person to be admitted to Harvard Law School without even formally applying.

Reggie Lewis initially struggled at Harvard Law School, but eventually found his stride and, through a securities law class, found his passion for corporate and business law. Following law school, he earned a position as a corporate associate with the prestigious New York firm Paul, Weiss, Rifkind, Wharton & Garrison. Remarkably, after only two years, Lewis decided he was ready to strike out on his own. Along with a young lawyer named Charles Clarkson, Lewis formed Lewis & Clarkson and set out building a successful Wall Street law firm.

Lewis possessed a tireless work ethic and was his firm's primary rainmaker. He pioneered a certain type of government-backed venture capital transaction for minority-owned businesses and eventually became nationally recognized for his work in that area. He also leveraged his network to increasingly earn business from clients that ordinarily worked with the whitest of white shoe New York law firms.

After fifteen years, Reggie Lewis had grown Lewis & Clarkson into a well-regarded Wall Street firm with an impressive, growing roster of clients. Nevertheless, Lewis yearned to do deals of his own and, to that end, formed TLC Group L.P., a private investment firm. His first big deal was the $22.5 million acquisition of McCall Pattern Company in 1983. Lewis cobbled the deal together with just $1 million in equity, scraped together from a few friends. The rest of the purchase price was raised through debt and institutional investors. Although this was Lewis's first major deal, he successfully led a remarkable resurgence of the company. When the company was sold several years later, Lewis produced a 90–1 return for his investors. In other words, the 80 percent of the equity of the company that he controlled (based on the $1 million in capital) was worth $90 million when the company was sold.

In 1987, Lewis struck again, this time with the acquisition of Beatrice Foods for $985 million. Again, he relied heavily on leverage. Before the deal was closed, Lewis worked behind the scenes to arrange for the disposition of several Beatrice assets around the world, which would generate cash to pay down the debt he used to acquire the company. Within a short time, the company was generating nearly $2 billion in annual revenue, thus making Beatrice the first black-owned enterprise in America to generate more than $1 billion in annual sales.

Reggie Lewis's remarkable run was tragically cut short when he succumbed to brain cancer in 1993 at just fifty-one years old. To put this in perspective, in just ten years (1983 to 1993), this bold man from Baltimore went from a modestly successful, independent Wall Street lawyer to the billionaire leader of a global conglomerate. Only in America!

Reggie Lewis's accomplishments warrant far more recognition and attention than they have received. In fact, until I started doing research for this book, I had never heard of him (and I suspect that many of you may not have not heard of him either). Any excuse one could possibly think of as to why he or she cannot escape the traditional path in the practice of law in favor of entrepreneurship can be immediately dismissed by considering what Reginald Lewis overcame.

He was an African American man from a lower-middle-class family in Baltimore. He worked incredibly hard to earn success in college and law school, and gained entry to an exclusive Wall Street law firm in the racially divisive 1960s. After only two years in practice, he started his own law firm and generated enough business to support himself and a small team of enterprising lawyers. If he had stopped there, the Reggie Lewis story would be worthy of a movie, but he was just getting started! In the clubby world of 1980s high finance, he shattered stereotypes and overcame latent racism to acquire two companies and, in the process, delivered fantastic returns for his investors and made himself a billionaire.

When he left Harvard for New York, Reggie Lewis didn't have a rich family or a deep network of wealthy friends who could set him up in business. Rather, he relied on his Alpha Characteristics to out hustle and out work his competition and overcome obstacles (and there were many) that stood in his way. Reggie Lewis had a clear vision of what his business life would look like, and he did not let anything keep him from accomplishing his goals. Had Lewis not died at such a young age, there can be little doubt that he would still be in the game and would be considered one of the greatest financiers and buyout kings in the history of American business.

DAVID RUBENSTEIN—CARLYLE GROUP

David Rubenstein has a remarkably similar background and trajectory as Reggie Lewis. He was born in 1949, seven years after Reggie Lewis, and lived in a working-class Jewish neighborhood in Baltimore. Rubenstein's father (who worked for the United States Postal Service) and mother (a homemaker) encouraged their son to maximize his potential through education.

Despite his working-class roots, Rubenstein earned his way into the exclusive Baltimore City College Prep school. Through superior academic performance, he earned scholarships to Duke University, where he earned his B.A. in 1970, and the University of Chicago Law School, where he earned his JD in 1973. As with Reggie Lewis, Rubenstein worked for Paul, Weiss in New York for two years (1973 to 1975). From there, the paths of Lewis and Rubenstein diverge, but ultimately merge once again.

After leaving Paul, Weiss, Rubenstein went to Washington, D.C. He worked as counsel to a United States Senate committee and then as a deputy domestic policy advisor to President Jimmy Carter. During his brief stint in government, Rubenstein was recognized for his dogged work ethic and general brilliance. After leaving the government world, Rubenstein went back into private law practice, but he was slowly coming to terms with the fact that he was not cut out for life in a law firm. Rather, he wanted to do something entrepreneurial and be his own boss. He continued to practice law over the next few years as he laid the groundwork for his escape.

Although he lacked any direct experience in business, in 1986, Rubenstein joined a few partners—including two other lawyers—and founded The Carlyle Group, a buyout firm that would target the acquisition of private companies. Over the next thirty years under Rubenstein's leadership, Carlyle grew from $5 million in capital and ten employees to a global investment firm with more than $140 billion in assets, 1,300 employees globally, and another 650,000 individuals employed by Carlyle's more than 200 portfolio companies. During that period, Carlyle has returned billions of dollars to its investors.

As with Reggie Lewis, the story of David Rubenstein shows that the circumstances into which people are born have very little to do with the things they can achieve if they couple a dynamic vision of the future with the grit and determination to succeed, no matter what may stand in their way. Rubenstein took advantage of the opportunities he earned and leveraged each successful accomplishment into new opportunities. Much like Lewis, Rubenstein used the practice of law to hone his deal-making chops, all the while laying the groundwork for his ultimate escape. Once he made his escape, Rubenstein relied on his many strong Alpha Characteristics to turn a relatively small amount of capital into a multi-billion-dollar global private equity firm.

DAVID BONDERMAN—TPG CAPITAL

David Bonderman, the co-founder of TPG Capital (formerly Texas Pacific Group), was born in Los Angeles in 1942, the son of a Russian immigrant. Bonderman is another Alpha who gained diverse experience early in his life and spent several years practicing law before making his escape into business. He earned his undergraduate degree from the University of Washington, and then made his way to Harvard Law School, where he graduated in 1966.

Following his graduation from Harvard, Bonderman traveled to Africa and also briefly spent time as an Assistant Professor at Tulane University School of Law. He then moved to Washington, D.C., where he served as a special assistant to United States Attorney General Ramsey Clark from 1968 to 1969. His interest in international affairs led to a fellowship with Harvard from 1969 to 1971, where he continued his studies in foreign and comparative law while based in Cairo, Egypt.

After gaining these valuable experiences, Bonderman decided to enter the private practice of law. He joined the prestigious firm Arnold & Porter in Washington, D.C. where he practiced from 1971 to 1983 and eventually earned partnership in the firm. Bonderman had a diverse practice that spanned corporate law, bankruptcy, securities, and antitrust. He developed deep experience negotiating deals and, in addition, became a well-regarded trial attorney.

In 1983, after twelve years practicing law with Arnold & Porter, Bonderman made his escape into business. First, he went to work with billionaire Robert Bass (where he also worked with Tom Barrack, profiled earlier in this book) and eventually served as COO of the Robert M. Bass Group, Inc. (now known as Keystone, Inc.). Bonderman invested in numerous deals and gained valuable deal-making experience during his tenure with the Bass Group, a family office for its billionaire founder. After almost ten immensely successful years with the Bass Group, Bonderman and his fellow Bass colleagues James Coulter and William S. Price, III left to found TPG. Since 1992, TPG has returned hundreds of millions (if not billions) of dollars to its investors through investments ranging from private equity to real estate to distressed debt, and most recently raised a $10.5-billion fund.

Bonderman is yet another example of an Alpha who successfully leveraged his diverse experience (international studies, government service, partner at a powerful D.C. law firm) and seized opportunity (the COO role with Bass) when it presented itself. Bonderman leveraged his strong negotiating skills to develop expertise as a master dealmaker, initially as an agent for Robert Bass, but later for himself and his investors. Bonderman was forty-one years old when he walked away from a lucrative partnership with Arnold & Porter, and was fifty when he started his own firm, TPG. Bonderman's escape from the practice of law into the world of business exemplifies the Alpha Characteristic of embracing risk and, in addition, demonstrates that it is never too late for one to make an escape.

JEROME KOHLBERG AND GEORGE ROBERTS—KOHLBERG KRAVIS & ROBERTS

Kohlberg Kravis & Roberts (KKR) is one of the most successful and highly-regarded private equity firms in the world. Henry Kravis is perhaps the best known of the three named partners, but his mentor Jerome Kohlberg and his cousin George Roberts, who were both lawyers, were equally instrumental in the rise of this American success story.

Jerome Kohlberg was born in New Rochelle, New York in 1925. Kohlberg served in the United States Navy during World War II, and after his service attended Swarthmore College on the G.I. Bill. After earning his undergraduate degree, Kohlberg went on to earn his MBA from Harvard and his law degree from Columbia University. After a brief stint in law, clerking for a Federal judge, Kohlberg joined the investment banking group at Bear Stearns. Kohlberg eventually became the head of corporate finance for Bear Stearns, and in the 1960s pioneered the early private equity investment model (then referred to as "bootstrap acquisitions").

George Roberts, who was nearly twenty years younger than Kohlberg, was raised in a Jewish family in Houston, Texas. Roberts attended high school at Culver Military Academy, and then earned his B.A. from Claremont McKenna College in 1966 and his law degree from the University of California Hastings College of Law in 1969. Roberts opted to forgo the practice of law altogether and joined his cousin Henry in the investment banking division of Bear Stearns, which is where he and Kravis met their mentor, Kohlberg.

As Roberts and Kravis learned the ins and outs of "bootstrap" transactions from Kohlberg, the trio put together a plan to form a leveraged buyout group within Bear Stearns. In 1976, when their LBO plan was turned down by the partners at Bear Stearns, the men decided over a dinner at Joe and Rose Restaurant in New York to start their own buyout firm.

With $5 million in capital (representing Kohlberg's entire nest egg) and an investment from Kravis's father, the three men launched Kohlberg, Kravis & Roberts. The firm has gone on to facilitate some of the greatest LBO and private equity transactions in the history of American business.

Although Kohlberg left the firm in 1987, due to differences with Roberts and Kravis over the strategic direction of the firm, KKR's dramatic success produced tremendous returns for its investors and made each of the men billionaires. While neither Kohlberg nor Roberts spent time directly in the practice of law, their legal training was critical to their ability to identify opportunities, assess risk, negotiate deals, and develop creative investment structures. While Kohlberg, Kravis, and Roberts each had sterling pedigrees and started KKR with significant financial resources (in Kohlberg's case, his personal nest egg earned over a long career at Bear Stearns, and in Kravis's and Roberts's cases, family wealth), they leveraged all of their resources and took on significant risk to maximize gains. Kohlberg was fifty-one years old when he struck out with the young cousins to start KKR, while Kravis and Roberts were in their mid-twenties, with only a few years' experience under their respective belts.

The paths taken by Kohlberg and Roberts are particularly instructive for readers who may be considering or currently attending law school. It can be a fantastic experience and provide a base of knowledge and skill that will serve the student well no matter what field the person ultimately pursues. As demonstrated by Kohlberg and Roberts, it is possible to make the jump immediately from law school to the business world. In each case, the men gained experience within a larger organization (Bear Stearns) before branching out on their own. At a minimum, those who are considering law school or currently attending law school as a path to earn a seat at the "deal table" should consider the paths taken by Kohlberg and Roberts as a viable alternative to the practice of law.

TEDDY FORSTMANN—FORSTMANN LITTLE & COMPANY

As noted earlier, Teddy Forstmann is one of my three business "mentors" profiled in this book. Forstmann was born into an upper-middle-class family, but the family business went bankrupt just as Teddy was reaching young adulthood. Notwithstanding this adversity, he set out on a colorful journey that would eventually lead him to the pinnacle of American business.

Teddy Forstmann was born in 1940 in Greenwich, Connecticut, the second of six children to Julius and Dorothy Forstmann. Julius ran a wool company that he had inherited from his father, who at one time had been one of the world's richest men. Unfortunately, in 1958 (when Teddy was eighteen years old), the family business went bankrupt. Nevertheless, Teddy was admitted to Yale University, where he earned his undergraduate degree and was a member of the men's hockey team. Forstmann was an average student at Yale, yet performed well enough to be admitted to law school at Columbia University. Due to the family's financial difficulties, Forstmann put himself through law school using his winnings from high-stakes bridge games.

After graduating from Columbia, Forstmann bounced around several small law firms in New York City, where he loosely focused his practice on corporate and securities law. About three years in, the firm with which Forstmann was associated earned a large Wall Street bond underwriting transaction. A senior partner at the firm selected Forstmann to be the firm's liaison with the printer on the deal, a task that Forstmann considered mind-numbing. Perhaps catching a glimpse of his future as a lawyer, it was this project that finally gave Forstmann the nudge he needed to walk away from the practice of law.

After escaping, Forstmann bounced around at a few smaller Wall Street investment houses, where he gained experience with stock underwritings and other financial transactions. At Fahaerty & Swartwood, he met and worked with Henry Kravis, who was also briefly with the firm. Kravis moved on to Bear Stearns, and Forstmann continued to bounce around from one small investment firm to another. Forstmann realized that he hated being stuck in an office and chafed under the structure and hierarchy of Wall Street firms. More importantly, he had the self-awareness to know that he would always be a terrible employee.

By 1974, at the age of thirty-four, Teddy Forstmann was out of work and nearly out of money. He sold some of his possessions and scraped together $20,000, which he determined gave him about a year's worth of living expenses, and thus about a year to figure out what to do next. While he was plotting his next move, he also continued to play high-stakes bridge games to hustle additional money and buy himself a little extra time.

During his last stint with a Wall Street investment firm, Forstmann worked with a Texas company called Graham Magnetics, which he had previously helped take public and ended up with a seat on the company's board of directors. During a meeting with Graham's chief executive officer, Forstmann expressed his belief that the time was right to take the company to market to find a buyer, and he convinced the CEO that he was the man to handle the transaction. He did not have a formal office or support team, but within eighteen months, he sold the company and earned himself a $300,000 fee.

Energized by his success as a quasi-investment banker, Forstmann set up shop in some extra space in his brother's office. From his new base of operations, he attempted to put together similar deals. In reality, though, Forstmann ended up spending an inordinate amount of time on the golf course and at the bridge table. At the same time, Forstmann's brother, Nick, was working with Henry Kravis at KKR. During a visit to their office, Forstmann met with Henry Kravis and Jerome Kohlberg, where they described to him the leveraged buyout transactions they were pursuing. Forstmann was intrigued and encouraged, as he had been mulling similar types of transactions himself.

Inspired by the meeting with KKR, Forstmann approached his golfing buddy, Derald Ruttenberg, the president of an industrial firm called Studebaker-Worthington, about attempting a leveraged buyout of Studebaker with KKR. Ruttenberg noted that the concept was akin to the transaction Forstmann had been pitching Ruttenberg for some time. So, he encouraged Forstmann to put the deal together himself, as opposed to working with KKR.

Forstmann accepted the challenge. With Ruttenberg's assistance, his brother Nick, and an investment banker friend named Brian Little, he formed his own buyout firm called Forstmann Little & Company. Forstmann Little went on to become one of the premier private equity/LBO firms of the 1980s, and over the ensuing decades, Forstmann became a billionaire. He went on to pursue big deals throughout the 1990s and early 2000s, until his untimely death in 2011 at the age of seventy-one.

Teddy Forstmann was a dynamic entrepreneur and financier. He gave the practice of law a shot, but clearly was not cut out for the buttoned-down life of a Wall Street lawyer. While he was probably better suited to the investment banking world, he still could not survive in a bureaucratic, hierarchical corporate environment. In other words, win or lose, he had to chart his own course. Perhaps through his forays into high stakes card games and hours spent on the links, Forstmann grew comfortable in his own skin and learned that his skills were better suited to putting deals together as a principal rather than agent. He was generous with his wealth during his life, and even in death (he is one of at least eight Alphas who made The Giving Pledge, through which wealthy individuals pledge to dedicate a majority of their wealth to charitable works).

Forstmann is a stellar example for young lawyers who are navigating the early years of their legal careers. Through his few years practicing, Forstmann no doubt gained important knowledge about the critical legal issues that arise in major financial transactions. While he bounced around the business world and did not last long working for others, he no doubt gained valuable expertise along the way, which would ultimately serve him well throughout his career.

What is most important in the Forstmann example, however, is his talent for pattern recognition and his ability to build and leverage his network. While Forstmann was figuring out what he would do with his life, he was putting the pieces together between his instincts about certain opportunities and transactions and what others were doing in the market (such as the team at KKR). He had confidence in his abilities, and had developed the connections and network to create and execute opportunities when the time was right.

TULLY FRIEDMAN—FRIEDMAN, FLEISCHMAN & LOWE

Tully Friedman is one of the pioneers of the private equity industry, particularly of the West Coast variety. He is one of a handful of Alphas who did not spend any significant amount of time practicing law, but rather went directly into finance. Friedman earned his undergraduate degree with great distinction from Stanford University, and then went on to earn his law degree from Harvard University.

Friedman started his career with Salomon Brothers, Inc. as an investment banker, where he eventually became a managing director and founded the firm's West Coast Corporate Finance Department. In 1984, Friedman joined forces with Warren Hellman, a former Lehman Brothers investment banker and founder of Hellman, Ferri Investment Associates (which eventually became the venture capital firm Matrix Management Company). From 1984 through 1997, Friedman's firm was involved in some of the most notable LBO and private equity transactions of the period, including deals involving Levi Strauss, Mattel, Young & Rubicam, and Franklin Resources.

In 1997, Friedman left Hellman & Friedman and, along with Spencer Fleischer, David Lowe, and Christopher Masto, founded Friedman, Fleischer & Lowe. They focused on smaller, middle market transactions, as opposed to the much larger deals that Hellman & Friedman was handling by then. Since its inception, the firm has raised more than $4.6 billion in equity commitments and has invested in companies such as Sealy Tempur-Pedic, Korn/Ferry, and Church's Chicken. FFL has been consistently ranked among the top private equity firms in the world (based on performance), including a #1 ranking in 2012.

Although he was one of the earlier pioneers of an industry that has deployed trillions of dollars in capital and created millions of jobs, Tully Friedman has maintained a relatively low profile. In conducting the research for this book, it was nearly impossible to find any information about his life prior to Salomon Brothers. Even after he achieved great success in business, the only personal information available about Mr. Friedman is connected to his charitable and avocational interests (such as his patronage of opera and the arts, and his role as co-chairman of conservative think tank American Enterprise Institute).

It is interesting to note that while some Alphas have written books or granted interviews and access to their business and personal lives, many profiled in this book are like Friedman—low key and prefer to retain relative anonymity and privacy. Nevertheless, Tully Friedman's accomplishments and contributions to an industry that has been a key piece of the American economic engine speak for themselves.

BENNO CHARLES SCHMIDT, SR.—J.H. WHITNEY & COMPANY

Benno Charles Schmidt, Sr. is another one of the pioneers of an industry (in this case, venture capital) who had an impact on global finance that will be felt well beyond his lifetime. Interestingly, Schmidt is credited with having coined the term "venture" capital, which grew out of shortening the word "adventure," which was the word Schmidt and his colleagues used to describe the wild nature of their investments. Perhaps more importantly, though, Schmidt is yet another example of one who overcame great personal adversity and leveraged his strong work ethic to maximize every opportunity presented to him.

Benno C. Schmidt, Sr. was born in Abilene, Texas on January 10, 1913. The family was not financially well off, a situation made worse after Schmidt's father passed away when Benno was just twelve years old. Although Schmidt did not have many material blessings, he believed that he had a privileged upbringing, in large part because his mother and members of his extended family put great emphasis on the importance of education and learning.

Schmidt stayed in Texas for college and law school, earning his law degree from UT in 1936. After graduating, Schmidt, who was one of the best students in the history of the University of Texas Law School, spent time teaching at both UT and Harvard Law School. However, as with many of the Alphas profiled in this book, Schmidt answered the call when his country needed him during World War II.

After the horrifying attack on Pearl Harbor, Schmidt enlisted in the United States Army. He eventually rose to the rank of colonel and was awarded several medals, including the Bronze Star. After completing his service at the end of the war, Schmidt served as general counsel to the economic division of the State Department, advising his colleagues on economic relations with Britain and other allies.

Soon, Schmidt would cross paths with John Hay "Jock" Whitney, one of the scions of the Whitney family, whose paternal grandfather was Secretary of the Navy under President Grover Cleveland and whose maternal grandfather had served Presidents Lincoln, McKinley, and Theodore Roosevelt. The Whitney family had amassed a fortune (mostly from investments in oil, tobacco, railway cars, and real estate), and Jock Whitney was charged with growing his share of the family fortune.

In 1946, Jock Whitney formed J. H. Whitney & Company with an initial investment of $10 million. His goal was providing capital to early-stage companies in emerging markets, and he asked Benno Schmidt to join him. Schmidt became a partner in J.H. Whitney & Company in 1946, and was named managing partner in 1960, a position he held until his retirement in 1992. During his tenure with the firm, J.H. Whitney & Company made many great investments. Perhaps the most famous of these is the firm's investment in Florida Foods Corporation, which developed several breakthrough products, including Minute Maid orange juice (eventually sold to the Coca Cola Company).

After losing his father when he was twelve years old, certainly no one would have blamed Schmidt if he had struggled to find his way in the world. Yet his mother, who worked as a secretary to support the family, instilled in Benno the vision that he was destined to achieve great things. With that support, he overcame adversity and committed himself to excellence. Due to his determination and commitment to play the long game, Schmidt's name will forever be synonymous with the industry he helped to create.

THOMAS JEFFERSON DAVIS, JR.—
DAVIS & ROCK AND THE MAYFIELD FUND

The final member of the duo of Alphas (along with Benno Schmidt, profiled above) who pioneered the venture capital industry is Tommy Davis, who earned massive success through his entre into the burgeoning venture capital industry—first with the eponymous Davis & Rock (which he founded with Arthur Rock in 1961) and then with Mayfield Fund (which he founded in 1969). As with several of the Alphas profiled in this book, Davis had diverse life experiences that served him well in his future business endeavors.

Davis was born in 1912 in Cincinnati, Ohio. He earned both his undergraduate and law degrees from Harvard University. He then served in the Office of Strategic Services behind Japanese lines in Burma during World War II, rising to the rank of captain in the United States Army.

Davis worked briefly as a lawyer for the National Labor Relations Board in San Francisco before he was recruited to serve as a Vice President of Kern County Land Company to diversify their investments beyond real estate, into corporate development opportunities. However, after deploying capital in a company called Watkins Johnson, the Kern County Land Company indicated a desire to be more cautious in terms of pursuing additional investments. Davis grew impatient and decided to strike out with the legendary Arthur Rock, an investment banker from the East Coast who had moved to California in 1961 to be closer to the emerging action of what would later be known as Silicon Valley.

The men formed Davis & Rock in 1961 with just $5 million in capital, which had been raised from a handful of high-net-worth individuals. The firm made investments in companies like Teledyne and Scientific Data Systems, which produced fantastic returns for their investors. Due to certain arcane securities laws at the time that would have made additional investments by the partnership challenging, the partners opted to amicably dissolve and go their separate ways. Nevertheless, the firm produced outstanding financial returns for its principals and their investors.

The same year Davis & Rock was dissolved, Tommy Davis founded Mayfield Fund, which has since raised nearly $4 billion in investor commitments across almost twenty funds during its forty-eight-year history. Picking up where he left off with Davis & Rock, Mayfield Fund has made numerous successful venture investments in companies like Compaq Computer, Genentech, Citrix, and Solarcity.

While Davis did not practice law for long, he brought a diverse set of experiences to the new world of venture capital investing. And, contrary to the stereotype that all lawyers are risk averse, both Benno Schmidt and Tommy Davis—two men who were lawyers before they did anything else professionally—were the ones who stepped up and pioneered an industry that deploys capital in companies with extremely high-risk profiles. One could argue that their legal education provided the framework to develop a methodology for adequately assessing those risks and the creativity to design a corresponding investment structure that appropriately rewards investors and principals.

* * *

The private equity (including LBO) and venture capital industries have been responsible for enormous economic growth and job and wealth creation in our country over the last several decades. While it is not surprising that men and women with backgrounds in law have participated in these industries with great success, it is perhaps a lesser known fact that some of the most successful firms and investments in these industries were created and executed by former lawyers. Some of the more colorful stories in this chapter (such as the rise of Reggie Lewis, David Rubenstein, and Teddy Forstmann) involve men who practiced law for several years and gained valuable experience before making their escape into the world of high finance. For any aspiring or newly minted lawyers who may be reading this book, the experiences of those profiled in this chapter should provide confidence that your law school years will not be wasted, even if you decide to move into an investment-related field in the future.

CHAPTER SIX

Wildcatters

_____

I f you enjoy reading about entrepreneurs and business stories involving unique individuals (particularly those who experience both the highest highs and the lowest lows), then you need look no further than the people who have built the oil, gas, and energy industry in the United States, sometimes referred to as "wildcatters." It has some of the most colorful personalities in any industry, and has probably produced more overnight millionaires (and in some cases, billionaires) than any other, including the current technology wave. One can find fascinating stories stretching back to the mid-1800s, as well as those involving modern-day explorers like Boone Pickens, Aubrey McClendon (who tragically passed away in 2016), and Harold Hamm.

In this chapter, we explore four lawyers who made the transition from practicing law to running billion-dollar oil, gas, and energy companies. As explored in Chapter Five, the belief that all lawyers are naturally risk-averse falls apart when one considers that these Alphas (and presumably other former lawyers who have not yet reached Alpha status) have escaped the law and earned success in one of the riskiest and most lucrative businesses in the world.

RICHARD KINDER—KINDER MORGAN, INC.

Richard Kinder was born in 1944 in Cape Girardeau, Missouri, where his father was an insurance salesman and his mother was a schoolteacher. Kinder attended the University of Missouri, where he earned both his undergraduate degree (in 1966) and his law degree (in 1968). The United States was fully engaged in the Vietnam War when Kinder graduated from law school, and so he selflessly chose to serve his country as a captain in the Army's Judge Advocate General (JAG) Corps.

After serving in the Army, Kinder returned home to Cape Girardeau, where he went into practice with a local law firm that had been founded by relatives of conservative talk-show host Rush Limbaugh (who is also a notable native of Cape Girardeau). As his experience practicing law grew, Kinder made one of his first entrepreneurial moves, investing in assets such as real estate, a bar, and a hotel. While Kinder's real estate investments were modestly successful, the hotel struggled and accordingly, the bank called the note, which Kinder and his wife had personally guaranteed. The result was a financial disaster. Kinder was highly leveraged and, in 1980, he and his then-wife were bankrupt. To his immense credit, however, with no legal responsibility to do so, Kinder eventually repaid every one of his debts more than twenty years after they had been discharged in bankruptcy.

One can easily imagine how personally devastating this period must have been for Kinder. He was a young man with a young family to support, and was likely questioning whether success would ever be in the cards for him. Fortunately, hope would come in the form of a call from an old college friend and future partner, Bill Morgan, regarding an opportunity to join Florida Natural Gas as its general counsel. About four years after Kinder joined, the company was acquired by Houston Natural Gas (later renamed Enron), whose CEO, Ken Lay, was another one of Kinder's college friends and a former colleague at Florida Natural Gas.

By 1990, Kinder had risen from general counsel of a regional natural gas company to president of Enron and the presumptive heir to Chairman and CEO Ken Lay. Six years later, Kinder believed that a succession plan was in place. He expected to become CEO while Lay would remain Chairman.

Instead, Kinder was betrayed by his longtime friend when, for reasons that are still not entirely clear, Lay and the company's board of directors decided to pass Kinder over for CEO. Therefore, in 1996, Kinder resigned from Enron. Although he probably did not see it this way at the time, this turned out to be an incredible blessing dressed up like another devastating defeat.

Kinder would not wait long for his next opportunity. His old friend Bill Morgan reached out again, this time with a proposition of a different sort. Morgan was making a play for some "old" assets that Enron was shedding in favor of its ill-fated energy trading business, and he wanted Kinder to join him.

What Kinder and Morgan accomplished from that point is the stuff of legends. Through Kinder Morgan, Inc., they acquired the cast-off assets from Enron for $40 million in 1996. As of 2017, that energy business controlled more than 84,000 miles of pipeline and had a market capitalization of nearly $43 billion! There are few companies or investments that have produced returns of that scale over a similar period.

Rich Kinder represents perhaps one of the most inspirational profiles in this book. Born and raised in a middle-class family in Missouri, Kinder earned two degrees from his home state university, and then served in the military for four years. He came back to work in a law firm in his hometown and took the risk to branch out from the practice of law and invest in some alternative assets. After making some good investments, he made one bad investment and based on that single failure, had to file for bankruptcy protection.

That is the point at which many people would give up the ghost of their entrepreneurial dreams and resign themselves to a life of minimal risk. But Kinder, with the help of his strong will and a network of friends he developed in college, picked himself up off the mat, slapped his gloves together, and stepped-to for the next round. He could have simply counted his blessings, kept his head down, and quietly shifted back into the relative safety of life as a lawyer. Instead, he leveraged his law degree to open access into a growing energy company and, once he regained his legs, moved into a front-line role in the business.

Kinder's willingness to swallow his pride and sharpen his focus on rebuilding from a professional low point provides a stark lesson for us all. Before taking an entrepreneurial step away from the practice of law, one should ask whether they are willing to go to zero. In other words, if everything that could possibly go wrong went wrong, would you be willing to lose everything from a material perspective? Whether on your own or with a spouse and family, would you pick up the pieces and start over? If the answer in your heart of hearts is a resounding "Yes!" (and as importantly, if you are married, if your spouse's response is also a resounding "Yes!"), then you should be willing to take a risk and step away from the practice of law and into the world of business. If, however, the answer is anything else, then perhaps you would be better off sticking to the practice of law, and maybe slowly branch out into other areas of business. That is a perfectly acceptable, even rational choice.

This is not to say that one should cavalierly make a gambler's choice to go all in (without a reasonable plan). Rather, one must accept that a possible outcome of entrepreneurial risk is that they might have to pick up the pieces and start over. Richard Kinder shows us that even after losing it all, with enough time and a willingness to sacrifice and work hard, it is possible to rebuild and earn a successful outcome. In addition, perhaps remembering how fleeting material things can be, Kinder has been very generous with his wealth (including, among other things, making The Giving Pledge).

TREVOR REES-JONES—CHIEF OIL & GAS

Trevor Rees-Jones is the quintessential modern-day wildcatter. Born in Texas in 1951, Rees-Jones is the grandson of a Presbyterian minister from Trefor, Wales who immigrated to the United States and pastored a church in Oklahoma. Trevor's father, Trevor William Rees-Jones, was a lawyer in Dallas, Texas with the firm Lock, Liddle & Sapp.

Trevor Rees-Jones earned his undergraduate degree at Dartmouth College, and then returned home to study law at Southern Methodist University. He began his legal career as a bankruptcy attorney at Thompson & Knight, later specializing further in oil and gas reorganization matters. After practicing law for five years, Rees-Jones realized that he was not cut out for a lifetime spent practicing law. Looking back, he noted that he was "more interested in putting deals together from a business standpoint: getting things done, getting wells drilled, finding a gas field, establishing production. I was just intrigued by that more than researching the law and writing briefs."

In 1984, with just $4,000 in his bank account and a $48,000 line of credit, Rees-Jones set out looking for oil and gas investment opportunities. At that point in his life, he was single and was willing to accept the tremendous risk that comes with the territory speculating in the world of oil and gas investments. By 1994, Rees-Jones had drilled more than 400 high-risk fields, and at one point suffered a gut-wrenching spell of seventeen dry holes in a row. Nevertheless, he persisted.

During this stretch, Rees-Jones literally went from boom to bust several times, but he loved every minute of it. When he was married in 1994, however, he decided to slightly scale back his risk. To that end, he founded Chief Oil & Gas along with a few other shareholders and a few hundred thousand dollars in capital. Over the next decade, Chief acquired several unconventional assets and utilized a new drilling technique called hydraulic fracturing (now commonly referred to as "fracking") to draw natural gas out of shale formations.

As a smaller, nimble oil and gas exploration outfit, Chief took chances with cutting-edge technology and riskier fields that larger competitors were not willing to take. Those risks paid off, as over the decade following its founding, Chief sold production, pipeline, and midstream assets to larger energy companies for billions of dollars. In the process, Rees-Jones built a reputation as a savvy negotiator and a world-class partner.

There is no doubt that, even though Trevor Rees-Jones realized that law was not his calling after only five years in practice, his experience with bankruptcy law (and particularly, restructurings and reorganizations involving oil and gas partnerships) was invaluable as he struck out on his own as a wildcatter. He developed a respect for risk, but was willing to analyze opportunities and tolerate the risk in exchange for an opportunity to earn above-market returns.

As with Richard Kinder, who could have given up after his personal bankruptcy, it would have been perfectly understandable if Rees-Jones had packed it in and shuffled back to Thompson & Knight after his losing streak of seventeen dry holes in a row. But instead, he redoubled his efforts, stayed the course, and has been rewarded handsomely for doing so.

JOSEPH CRAFT, III—ALLIANCE RESOURCE PARTNERS

Joe Craft was born in 1950 in the small town of Hazard, Kentucky, which was one of the poorest towns in Kentucky, whose fortunes turned due to its vast stores of coal. As with Trevor Rees-Jones, Craft's father—Joseph Craft, Jr.—was a lawyer in Hazard and the younger Craft would eventually follow his father's footsteps into the practice of law. As with Rich Kinder, Craft opted to pursue his education in his home state, earning his undergraduate degree in accounting (1972) and his law degree (1976), each from the University of Kentucky.

Initially, Craft went to law school with the intention of becoming a tax lawyer. However, after the energy crisis hit the US during the 1970s, he shifted his focus to working in the energy industry. Craft eventually took a job as a lawyer for a company called Falcon Coal, where his responsibilities reached beyond the law to include accounting, administrative matters, and land deals.

A decade removed from law school, Craft was recruited as general counsel of a company called Mapco, based in Tulsa, Oklahoma. Ten years later, Craft was president of Mapco's coal division, and eventually led a management buyout of the coal business, renaming it Alliance Resource Partners (ARP). Under Craft's leadership and unique approach to the business of coal mining, ARP has produced remarkable returns for its investors, created thousands of jobs, and become a powerful voice for the coal industry in what has become a politically charged environment.

While Craft did not follow the pattern of a typical "wildcatter," his path is one that many enterprising lawyers could emulate in a variety of industries. He identified an industry in which he thought there would be enormous opportunity and sought to build his knowledge and add value. He put in the time as general counsel for many years, but sought opportunities to branch out into other areas of the business (finance, acquisitions, etc.). Finally, when the time was right, he led the charge in executing a management buyout of the business he was running for Mapco. In 1999, after producing great results in the business, Craft took ARP public.

Craft entered an industry fraught with risk, but his legal experience allowed him to carefully analyze and assess the attendant risks before he transitioned from law to business. As with all the Alphas profiled in this book, Joe Craft applied his strong work ethic and a unique approach to his business to earn fantastic results. In addition, he has shared his success with others. Not only has he created high paying jobs that allow countless people to pursue their own dreams, but he has also given generously to the causes and institutions that are close to his heart (including making The Giving Pledge), thus providing opportunity to countless others.

RANDA WILLIAMS—ENTERPRISE PRODUCTS

Randa "Randy" Duncan Williams is one of only two Alpha women profiled in this book. Her father, Dan Duncan, was a serial entrepreneur in the energy business. He is most notable for Enterprise Products, a transportation company in the natural gas and oil industries that he founded in 1968 with just $10,000 and two propane delivery trucks. By 2010, Enterprise Products was a public company that controlled more than 48,000 miles of onshore and offshore pipeline assets. Remarkably, in just one generation Dan Duncan, who lost his mother when he was seven years old, lost his brother the same year, and lost his father (who was a farmer) when he was just seventeen, had become a billionaire.

In 2005, Duncan also founded Enterprise GP Holdings, a midstream (i.e., the part of the business between exploration and the end user) energy holding company based in Houston, Texas. Unfortunately, in 2010, Duncan passed away due to a cerebral hemorrhage at the age of seventy-seven. During that brief window in 2010, the estate tax law had been repealed (but not yet replaced) and, as such, Duncan became the first (and probably last) billionaire to pay no federal estate tax upon his death. As such, each of his children, including his daughter Randy Williams, became billionaires themselves.

As with others we have profiled in this book who were born into or inherited great wealth, Randy Williams could have easily sat back and lived off the wealth created by her father. Instead, she set out to stake her own claim in the world and, in the process, has continued the legacy created by her father.

Randy Williams earned her undergraduate degree from Rice University in 1985 and her law degree from the University of Houston in 1988. Following her graduation from law school, she practiced law with two different firms in Houston: Butler & Binion and Brown, Sims, Wise & White. She focused on areas such as toxic torts, maritime law, and other litigation matters. After nearly six years, she joined the family business (Enterprise Products) as a vice president, and by 2001, had worked her way up to president and CEO of the company. In 2007, she was named co-chairman of the company. All told, she has been responsible for leading the company's growth for more than 20 years.

Again, not one of us chooses the circumstances into which we are born. Dan Duncan and his wife, Jan, clearly impressed upon their children the importance of being responsible with their wealth and giving generously from their bounty. In Randa's case, she enthusiastically took on the mantle of leading Enterprise Products after her father's death in 2010. While she did not share the hardscrabble beginnings that likely motivated her father's rise to success, Williams was driven by a desire to carry on her family's legacy of business growth and philanthropy. While her legal background was not directly related to the family's business interests, her analytical ability and organizational skills no doubt served her well in her professional capacity with Enterprise and her role as trustee of the various entities that control the family assets.

* * *

While not all the individuals profiled in this chapter are "wildcatters" in to purest sense of the word, they each walked away from the relative safety of the practice of law to enter the risky world of the energy business. They each leveraged their legal training, along with other diverse experiences, to build valuable businesses, create thousands of jobs, and return billions of dollars to investors. Moreover, in the process of making themselves extremely wealthy, they have also used their wealth to provide a hand up to those less fortunate, and improve our culture by supporting the arts and other institutions that influence culture and provide opportunities to many.

CHAPTER SEVEN

Masters of the Universe

———

Throughout this book, we have profiled people who have escaped law into the diverse fields of industry, real estate, private equity, venture capital, and energy. In each case, those entrepreneurs allocated capital to operating entities or assets and, through their direct efforts, influenced the operations of their respective businesses to maximize value. In this chapter, we profile individuals who also allocate capital, but they do so one level up from the other entrepreneurs we have studied thus far. In other words, the men profiled in this chapter allocate capital based on certain trading strategies or special situations and seek to produce returns based on the spread between the value when they buy and the value when they sell those assets. Rather than taking an active role in directing the operations of a specific business or asset, the entrepreneurs that you will read about in this chapter leverage their superior analytical skills to identify patterns and execute often complex trading strategies to produce above-market returns.

ROBERT D. ZIFF—ZIFF BROTHERS INVESTMENTS

In the current environment of populist rage against the wealthy, it is perhaps easiest for those who resent such people to reserve their most cynical outlook for those who inherit billions of dollars. Notwithstanding the fact that in most of those cases, someone in those families legitimately earned the money along the way (often with their blood, sweat, and tears), paid tens (or hundreds) of millions of dollars in taxes, created jobs, and generously supported charitable causes, those who inherit great wealth are rarely given much credit, even when they are good stewards of their inheritance. The story of Robert Ziff should serve to change that perception.

Robert Ziff's father, William B. Ziff, Jr., was himself the heir of the publishing company Ziff Davis, Inc., which his father (William Ziff, Sr.) founded in 1927 with partner Bernard Davis. After his father's death in 1953, William Ziff returned to the United States from Germany, where he was studying philosophy, to assume leadership of the family business. One of his first moves was to buy out his father's partner. After that, he redirected the focus of the company toward specialized niche markets such as computers, photography, and automotive. This proved to be highly attractive to advertisers, who loved the ability to specifically target qualified customers.

By the early 1990s, William Ziff, Jr. expressed his desire for his sons, Robert, Dirk, and Daniel, to take over the business when he was ready to move on. After a few years of contemplation and discussion, however, the brothers decided that they were not interested in taking on the Ziff Davis business, and so their father sold the company to Forstmann Little in 1994 for $1.4 billion.

It would have been simple enough for the story to end here. But instead, Robert Ziff and his brothers formed Ziff Brothers Investments with the goal of actively investing their wealth across a wide variety of asset classes, including equities, debt, real estate, commodities, private equity, and hedge funds. In addition, the firm provided an initial seed investment of $100 million to Daniel Och for an interest in hedge fund Och-Ziff Capital Management.

Robert Ziff attended Harvard University, where he earned his bachelor's degree, with honors, in electrical and computer engineering. He went on to earn his law degree from Cornell University and clerked for Chief Judge Monroe McKay of the Tenth Circuit Court of Appeals following his graduation. Likewise, his brothers have earned degrees from Ivy League institutions and, together, they took seriously their obligation to be good stewards of the wealth they inherited. Not only have they successfully preserved that wealth, but through the myriad investment strategies they have pursued over the last twenty years or so, they have grown those assets nearly ten times, to over $12 billion.

As with many individuals who inherit significant wealth, Robert Ziff could have delegated management of the family inheritance to an army of wealth managers and simply lived off the annual distributions. Instead, Ziff earned his law degree, has contributed his analytical and organizational skills to his family investment firm, and has participated in generating outstanding results. The brothers, through their investments and returns, have no doubt generated jobs and wealth for others and have continued the family tradition of active philanthropy.

BRUCE KARSH—OAKTREE CAPITAL MANAGEMENT

Bruce Karsh was born in 1955 and raised in St. Louis, Missouri. He earned his undergraduate degree from Duke University in 1977 and his law degree from the University of Virginia in 1980. Following his graduation from law school, Karsh clerked for Justice Anthony Kennedy, who was then an appellate court judge on the Ninth Circuit Court of Appeals.

After his clerkship, Karsh worked briefly for the well-respected firm O'Melveny & Meyers, where he gained experience in its corporate finance practice group. He was then recruited to become an assistant to Eli Broad, Chairman of SunLife Insurance Company and SunAmerica. Through his work with SunLife, Karsh met a man named Howard Marks, who was at that time a senior executive with TCW Group, an asset management firm.

In the late 1980s, Marks recruited Karsh to join TCW to lead its distressed debt investments practice. Eight years later, Karsh, Marks, and three other TCW employees founded Oaktree Capital Management, a global alternative investment management firm. Essentially, Oaktree investors hire Bruce Karsh and his colleagues to make investment decisions about how to allocate capital among such assets as corporate debt, public securities, convertible securities, real estate funds, and distressed debt.

Karsh's legal experience has provided a solid framework through which he has developed a sterling track record of profitably assessing and executing investments in distressed debt situations). Moreover, considering the backgrounds of many members of the Oaktree team, Karsh values the perspective brought to their business by those with a legal background. Indeed, of the five-person board of directors, three of its members (including Karsh) have law degrees, and each of those men spent significant time practicing law before making their respective escapes.

Karsh illustrates many of the most important Alpha Characteristics. His diligent work ethic resulted in outstanding academic results, which led to an elite clerkship and a job with a top corporate law firm. Through his position at SunLife, he leveraged his network and was recruited to his next opportunity, a position outside of the law as a distressed debt investor. After learning the ropes of his new business, he partnered with a core team and launched his own firm. His willingness to leave behind the prestige of the well-respected law firm was perhaps the first demonstration of his ability to manage and thrive upon risk. His remarkable success in the business of distressed debt investing represents yet another blow to the stereotype of the perpetually risk-averse lawyer. To the contrary, it appears that Karsh's success in business is due in large part to the critical skills (attention to detail, synthesizing a high volume of information in a short amount of time, analyzing risk and opportunities, and translating them into creative solutions) that he no doubt refined during law school and his time spent in the practice of law.

PAUL E. SINGER—ELLIOTT MANAGEMENT CORPORATION

Paul Singer was born in Manhattan in 1944, where he was raised by his pharmacist father and homemaker mother. Singer earned his undergraduate degree from the University of Rochester in 1966, and his law degree from Harvard University in 1969. After spending a few years working for corporate law firms, he earned a position as a real estate lawyer with the investment banking firm Donaldson Lufkin & Jennrette. Later, with the backing of $1.3 million he raised from friends and family, Singer left DLJ and started Elliott Management Corporation (after his middle name) to pursue investment opportunities in distressed debt situations. Since founding Elliott Management Corp, Singer has produced returns that dwarf the total capital invested.

As with Bruce Karsh, Paul Singer has leveraged his legal background to generate market busting returns in distressed debt transactions. In fact, *Fortune* has referred to him "one of the smartest and toughest money managers" in the hedge fund business. He has developed a special expertise in buying sovereign debt (the debt of another nation) at a steep discount, and then collecting all (or nearly all) of the original principal amount of that debt, plus interest, by investing in the legal process of enforcing his rights as a creditor. While he only practiced law for a few years, Singer has leveraged his experience and knowledge of the legal process to give his firm an edge in this highly profitable subset of the hedge fund industry.

Singer is now a multi-billionaire who gives generously to a variety of causes, including The Giving Pledge, various educational organizations, the arts, police and military organizations, and Jewish and Christian religious organizations based in Israel. Singer is yet another Alpha who busts the "anti-risk" image that haunts most lawyers, and has exhibited many other Alpha Characteristics on his way to massive success.

CRAIG COGUT—PEGASUS CAPITAL ADVISORS

Craig Cogut has followed an interesting path from practicing lawyer to entrepreneur, creating two well-respected investment firms: Apollo Global Management and Pegasus Capital Advisors. The early years of Cogut's journey mirror the path blazed by many other Alphas. Cogut earned his undergraduate degree from Brown University and his law degree from Harvard, and then started his journey in a rather traditional manner.

Cogut began his career with the well-regarded West Coast firm of Irell & Manella, where he practiced from 1979 to 1984. During the '80s, Drexel Burnham Lambert was perhaps the hottest investment bank in the world, known for its specialty of raising money though high-yield "junk bonds" to finance management buyout transactions. Cogut earned a role as a trusted counselor to Michael Milken and spent six years as an advisor to Drexel. It was during this time that Cogut developed new skills and branched out from his role as legal counsel.

When Drexel ran into trouble as the result of some of its transactions in the late 1980s, Cogut and several other colleagues from Drexel formed Apollo Global Management, an alternative asset management firm with a specialty in distressed debt and complex restructuring transactions. It was here that Cogut honed his investment skills and fully transitioned away from his role as "just a lawyer."

In 1995, Cogut left Apollo and formed Pegasus Capital Advisors, another alternative investment firm focused on making investments in middle market companies in distressed situations and turning them around. Since its founding, Pegasus has deployed more than $2 billion in capital, producing fantastic returns for its investors. Through the expertise of its team, Pegasus has taken companies once on the brink and turned them around, in the process saving jobs and creating wealth for many employees and members of management who participated in those turnarounds.

Cogut is a great example of a lawyer who filled a specific market need by leveraging his legal expertise and then, when opportunity presented itself, acquiring the skill of analyzing and executing high-risk (and high-reward) distressed debt investments. His escape from law took time, but he methodically transitioned from well-regarded law firm, to high-energy investment bank, to co-founding a global asset management firm, and then finally running his own shop. As with Bruce Karsh of Oaktree Capital Management, Cogut seemingly attributes value to legal experience when it comes to successful distressed debt investing, as four of the fourteen members of his firm's investment team—including Cogut himself—have law degrees and spent some time practicing law before moving into the business side of the investment world.

* * *

The hedge fund and alternative asset investment world is one replete with highly intelligent, analytical people who possess the valuable skill of seeing value and opportunity where others only see trouble. Even the most successful investors in that world make mistakes, but they are right more often than they are wrong. And perhaps most importantly, sometimes they are right in very big ways—meaning the return on investment from their "winners" is often well above the returns that can be earned in just about any other asset class. The men profiled in this chapter demonstrate that the skills one develops in law school and through the practice of law can prove invaluable in certain types of business, including those with extreme risk profiles. Three of the four Alphas profiled in this chapter focus almost exclusively on investing in distressed debt and restructuring situations, which require a deep understanding of the legal process (particularly bankruptcy and creditor's rights) to fully assess risk and opportunity. While there are many highly successful distressed debt investors who do not have a legal background, those who have experience in law possess an edge when it comes to analyzing those investments.

CHAPTER EIGHT

In the Arena

One of the things that would appear on many of our respective lists of "what I would do if I had a billion dollars" is own a professional sports team. Personally, I can think of few things that would be more fun than owning an NFL franchise, and many entrepreneurs (perhaps most notably, marketing guru Gary Vaynerchuk) make no secret of their goal of owning a professional sports team one day. (In Gary's case, he has set his sights on one day owning his beloved New York Jets.) In this chapter, we profile seven Alphas who transitioned from law to business and, after maximizing value and reaching billionaire status, acquired a professional sports team. In some cases, these individuals lead a consortium of investors in an ownership group. In one instance, the individual lost his team after being recorded making vile, racially charged comments. Nevertheless, each of these Alphas demonstrate the possibilities one could pursue after making a successful escape from the practice of law to the world of business.

DAN GILBERT—QUICKEN LOANS (CLEVELAND CAVALIERS)

Of all the Alphas profiled in this book, Dan Gilbert is perhaps the most entrepreneurial or, stated differently, the least lawyer-like. Gilbert was born in Detroit, Michigan in 1962. He was raised in an entrepreneurial family and pursued various business adventures from a very early age, including making and selling pizzas in his neighborhood (much to the chagrin of a local pizza shop that lost business to the upstart entrepreneur). Gilbert stayed in Michigan for his schooling, earning his undergraduate degree in journalism from Michigan State University, and his law degree from Wayne State University.

Building on his early forays into business, while he was in college, Gilbert earned his real estate license and went to work in his family's Century 21 real estate agency. Although he earned his law degree and was admitted to the Michigan Bar, Gilbert always seemed to be moving toward running his own show. After selling homes and earning commissions, Gilbert began to realize that there was more money in originating mortgages than selling homes. So, in 1985, he and a few partners (including his brother, Gary) formed Rock Financial.

The company grew to include more than twenty brick and mortar sites. But as Rock passed its first decade in business, Gilbert anticipated the incredible opportunities presented by the digital age and led the company in a move to the online environment. The business took off and in 2000, Gilbert sold the company to Intuit for more than half a billion dollars, which renamed it Quicken Loans, after its flagship accounting software. Interestingly, Intuit was unable to integrate the business into its broader Quicken platform, and so Gilbert led a buyout of the business from Intuit just two years later at a fraction of the original sale price.

Through his success with Quicken Loans and Rock Financial, Gilbert has also become a successful real estate investor (primarily in Detroit), a great supporter of startup communities, and a well-respected philanthropist. In 2005, he leveraged all his business acumen and resources to lead an investor group in its acquisition of the Cleveland Cavaliers from its previous owner. When the deal was announced, Gilbert was quick to reassure fans that he had no plans to move the team out of the city. He went further to promise the fans that his intention was to leverage his business experience to build a world-class franchise and bring a championship to the city. Gilbert has not only delivered on his promise of an NBA Championship, but has also built a perennial contender and increased the value of the franchise significantly over the last decade.

Although Gilbert did not spend time practicing law, it would be foolish to assume that he has not valued and used his legal education in building successful businesses. One could conclude that Gilbert's ability to be successful in so many different areas of business (real estate, mortgage loans, venture capital, and sports) is at least in part due to the skills he developed in law school—particularly the ability to break things down into their simplest parts, put them back together into a cohesive story and then methodically execute a clear strategy. Gilbert clearly possesses many of the Alpha Characteristics that contribute to success for those who transition from law to businesses: he was born into a tight, entrepreneurial family; his educational pedigree mattered very little to his ultimate success; money was not his primary motivation (he has stated that entrepreneurship is about building things of value, not chasing money); he has exhibited a tolerance for, and ability to manage, risk; he has developed diverse experience in a variety of businesses; and he is playing the long game and paying it forward (by, among other things, making The Giving Pledge). This last point is also demonstrated by his belief in the ability to turn the Cavaliers franchise into a championship team, and his investments in the City of Detroit when all others were running away.

STEPHEN ROSS—THE RELATED COMPANIES (MIAMI DOLPHINS)

Stephen Ross is another proud native son of Michigan, born in Detroit in 1940. Like Gilbert, Ross stayed in his home state as he pursued higher education, graduating from the University of Michigan with a degree in accounting in 1962 and earning his law degree from Wayne State University in 1965. Ross left Michigan for New York in 1966, where he earned his LLM in Tax from the prestigious graduate tax program at New York University.

Ross returned home and began his career in law as a tax attorney with Coopers & Lybrand in Detroit. By 1968, however, he went back to New York, accepting a position with real estate company Laird, Inc. He diversified his experience through his work with Laird, and then moved on to the corporate finance department of Bear Stearns, where he augmented his background in tax with experience financing complex transactions.

In 1972, Ross was ready to step out on his own. With just a $10,000 loan from his mother, Ross started a business that leveraged his deep knowledge of federal tax law and designed creative investment vehicles. They allowed high-net worth investors to shelter income based on generous terms made available by the federal government to promote certain types of investments that benefited low-income communities. Ross was extremely successful creating these structures, and soon started to branch out into real estate development projects.

Later that same year, Ross founded The Related Companies, a real estate development company. Over the last forty-five years, the company has successfully executed real estate projects throughout the world. It now directly employs more than 2,000 people and controls assets collectively valued at more than $15 billion. The company has recently expanded into adjacent businesses through its ownership interests in companies like Equinox (a chain of high-end fitness clubs) and Union Square Events (a large event management and catering firm).

In 2009, Ross completed the acquisition of a 95 percent interest in the Miami Dolphins franchise, stadium, and surrounding land from entrepreneur Wayne Huizenga for more than $1 billion. Since acquiring control of the team, Ross has brought on some high-profile partners, including Serena and Venus Williams, Marc Anthony, and Gloria Estefan. Through his entrée into the sports world, Ross also co-founded RSE Ventures in 2012. This firm invests in cutting-edge technologies that will impact the sports and entertainment world in the years to come.

Stephen Ross is yet another Alpha who leveraged his particular expertise in the law to develop creative solutions and deliver tremendous value to high net worth investors. Based on his early success bridging the gap between law and business, Ross struck out on his own and over more than forty years, he built a multi-billion-dollar real estate firm. Ross has also demonstrated incredible generosity, and is one of the Alphas to have made The Giving Pledge. Now, following in the footsteps of fellow Michigan native Dan Gilbert, Ross is the owner of a high-profile professional football team and is making smaller investments in technologies that could one day transform that industry.

TED LERNER—LERNER ENTERPRISES
(WASHINGTON NATIONALS)

The story of Ted Lerner is quintessentially representative of the limitless possibilities made available to those with pluck and a willingness to patiently build over time. Lerner was born in 1925 in the northwest corner of Washington, D.C. to Orthodox Jewish parents, Mayer and Ethel, who immigrated to the United States from Palestine and Lithuania, respectively, in search of a better life. Ted Lerner had a middle-class upbringing. Perhaps foreshadowing his future move into sports, he showed early entrepreneurial spunk by selling magazines door to door to earn money to watch Washington Senators baseball games from the bleacher seats. As with many men of his generation, Lerner answered the call when his country needed him, and served in an administrative role with the United States Army during World War II.

After the war, Lerner returned home and earned his undergraduate and law degrees from George Washington University, which he paid for in part through the assistance of the G.I. Bill. As Dan Gilbert would do many years later, Lerner sold homes in his spare time during law school, which piqued his interest in real estate. After graduating, Lerner spent only a year practicing law before he decided to make his escape. After being stiffed by a client for work he had dutifully performed, Lerner believed there had to be a better way to make a living.

In 1952, with just $250 in startup capital (which he borrowed from his wife), Lerner and his wife, Annette, founded Lerner Enterprises, with the goal of building a successful family business that they might one day pass on to their children. While Ted and Annette were the majority shareholders, Ted's brother, Larry, was a minority shareholder, an officer, and director of the company.

Ted Lerner and Lerner Enterprises sold roughly 22,000 homes over almost a decade before he decided to branch out into developing real estate projects on his own. In 1960, just eight years after starting his company, Lerner pulled off what might be one of the greatest acquisitions on the East Coast in the last fifty years. Lerner Enterprises acquired two large tracts of land in an area known as Tysons Corner, Virginia, and developed what would become the epicenter of the business community in suburban D.C. Today Lerner Enterprises is the largest private landowner in the metro D.C. market.

Unfortunately, in 1983, Ted and Lawrence had a falling out, and Ted removed Larry from his role as an officer and director of the company. The dispute led to litigation in Maryland, which was initially resolved with Ted maintaining operating control of the business, and Larry holding on to his stock with the right to receive distributions *pari passu* with Ted. As with many family businesses, tensions between one generation and another or members of the same generation (siblings, cousins, etc.) often result in the end of the business, not to mention heartbreaking splits that tear the fabric of the family. In the case of Lerner Enterprises, while Ted and his brother have battled in and out of court for more than thirty years, the business has not only survived, but thrived through it all.

Thanks to the vast wealth created through Lerner Enterprises' real estate development projects, Ted Lerner, his son, and two sons-in-law made the winning bid to acquire the Washington Nationals baseball franchise from Major League Baseball in 2006. In just a little more than a decade after acquiring the team, the Lerners (who own 90 percent of the franchise) turned the Nationals into a playoff team and a legitimate World Series contender. The Lerner family is also a partner in an investment partnership called Monumental Sports & Entertainment, which owns interests in the Washington Capitals (of the NHL), Washington Wizards (of the NBA), and Washington Mystics (of the WNBA).

At the age of ninety-one, Lerner is still active in his various business interests, and he and his wife have realized their dream of seeing their children involved in the family business. As an Alpha, Lerner's life demonstrates the immense value of having strong family ties and an entrepreneurial background early in life. After serving his country, Lerner took advantage of the opportunities afforded him through the G.I. Bill to earn his law degree, and then quickly diversified his experience outside the practice of law and into the real estate business. His life demonstrates the value of playing the long game, as he is still driving hard and has overcome adversity along the way. Ted Lerner's legal background provided a platform through which he has earned massive success in business, realized his dream of creating a multigenerational family enterprise, and has successfully moved into the world of sports. Not bad, going from the bleacher seats to the owner's box in a lifetime!

MARC LASRY—AVENUE CAPITAL (MILWAUKEE BUCKS)

Marc Lasry was born in Morocco in 1959, and immigrated to the United States with his family when he was just seven years old. Lasry's father, Moise, was a computer programmer and his mother, Elise, was a schoolteacher. The family lived a traditionally middle-class life in West Hartford, Connecticut. After high school, Lasry earned his undergraduate degree from Clark University in 1981 and his law degree from New York Law School in 1984.

During law school, Lasry gained experience working with a bankruptcy court judge, and then practiced briefly as a bankruptcy lawyer with the firm Angel & Frankel. Lasry left and joined a firm called R.D. Smith, where he learned the business of acquiring unsecured claims on behalf of investors. In 1987, he joined Cowen & Company, where he was a co-director of the firm's bankruptcy and reorganization business.

While at Cowan & Company, Lasry caught the attention of billionaire Robert Bass, a client of the firm. Bass has a fantastic eye for talent—as the reader may recall, he also backed Tom Barrack and David Bonderman, who were profiled in Chapters Four and Five, respectively. In 1989, when Lasry was just five years out of law school, Bass staked him and his sister, Sonia Gardner (also a lawyer), with $100 million. The siblings formed Amroc Investments, which invested in distressed debt and restructuring transactions. After winding up Amroc roughly five years later, the brother-sister team founded Avenue Capital Group with just an initial investment of $10 million of their own capital. Since founding Avenue Capital, Lasry has deployed billions of dollars in capital both domestically and internationally in distressed opportunities. He has been quoted as saying that they like to focus on great companies with terrible balance sheets. He has produced fantastic returns for his investors and made himself a billionaire.

In 2014, Lasry (along with a partner, Wesley Edens, who is also a hedge fund investor with Fortress Investment Group) acquired the Milwaukee Bucks for more than $500 million and set out to turn the franchise into a contender. At the time of the acquisition, Lasry and Edens committed to keep the team in Milwaukee, invest $100 million in a new arena, and bring their business acumen to the franchise to build a winning organization. Just three years after buying the team, Lasry and Edens had the Bucks back on track—the team was above .500 in the 2016-2017 season and made the playoffs (losing in the first round to the Toronto Raptors).

As with many other Alphas profiled in this book, particularly those who built their wealth through hedge funds and investing in distressed debt, Lasry directly leveraged his legal expertise to transition from practicing bankruptcy law to analyzing and executing transactions involving distressed companies. He seized opportunities when presented and delivered tremendous value for others on his way to earning fantastic personal success. Having now moved into the world of professional sports, Lasry's diverse experience and legal background will no doubt continue to serve him well.

MARK WALTER—GUGGENHEIM PARTNERS (L.A. DODGERS)

Mark Walter is another Alpha who is a poster child for the American Dream. He was born in Cedar Rapids, Iowa in 1960, where he grew up in a middle-class town. Walter's father, Ed, supported the family by manufacturing concrete blocks. Mark learned the value of hard work early in his life at a gas station, earning enough money to buy himself a car.

Walter earned his undergraduate degree from Creighton University, and then moved on to Northwestern University for his law degree. After graduating, Walter briefly practiced law with the Chicago firm Sonnenschein Carlin Nath & Rosenthal (now SNR Denton) before moving on to the investment banking group of First Chicago Bank (now part of JP Morgan Chase). After leaving First Chicago Bank, Walter founded Liberty Hampshire Co., a boutique investment firm that is now a subsidiary of Guggenheim.

Today, Walter is the CEO of Guggenheim, which manages more than $200 billion in assets and has diverse investments in insurance companies, distressed securities, real estate, and other assets. When the L.A. Dodgers franchise came on the market due to the financial disaster facing its then-owner Frank McCourt, Walter put together a consortium of investors that included Magic Johnson and put forward the prevailing bid of over $2 billion for the storied franchise. Under Walter's leadership as Chairman of the team, the Dodgers have risen back to prominence. They were a step away from the World Series in 2016, losing to the eventual World Series Champion Chicago Cubs in game six of the National League Championship Series.

The pattern that should by now be clear is exemplified again with Mark Walter. He applied his diligent work ethic and earned admission to law school. After briefly practicing law with a top firm, he made his escape into business, first into investment banking and then into investing in distressed debt. Having earned massive success in the hedge fund world, Walter seized the opportunity to acquire an iconic Major League Baseball franchise, which he believed was undervalued and could be turned around. Although the worlds of high finance and sports are quite different, the disciplines that Walter developed and executed to earn success with Guggenheim have thus far served him and his co-investors well—not to mention Dodgers players and fans, as the franchise is back on top in the league.

DONALD STERLING—REAL ESTATE INVESTOR (FORMER OWNER OF L.A. CLIPPERS)

Donald Sterling was born in Chicago, Illinois in 1934 to Jewish immigrants. Sterling's family moved to Los Angeles when he was two years old, and he earned his undergraduate degree from California State University, Los Angeles in 1956. Four years later, he earned his law degree from Southwestern Law School in Los Angeles. The family surname was Tokowitz, which Donald legally changed to Sterling in 1959 when he was twenty-five years old, believing that it was too difficult to pronounce and the reason he faced antisemitism in the legal and business world was at least partly due to his last name.

When Sterling graduated from law school in 1960, there were not many opportunities with large Los Angeles law firms for Jewish men, and so Sterling set out on his own, practicing in the areas of family law and personal injury. Almost immediately after starting his law practice, Sterling also started investing in real estate, buying multi-unit apartment properties one at a time. As his real estate empire grew, he added variety to his holdings, including several high-value commercial properties. Eventually, he transitioned from the practice of law to exclusively running his real estate empire.

In 1981, Sterling bought the San Diego Clippers of the National Basketball Association for $12.5 million. He moved the team to Los Angeles in 1984, but during most of the thirty years Sterling owned the franchise, the team consistently underperformed and Sterling was widely considered one of the worst owners in all of sports. At one point, the NBA required that Sterling hire a professional manager or risk losing the franchise. Sterling complied, and the team improved slightly thereafter.

Sterling's troubled tenure as the owner of the Clippers came to a disturbing end when he was caught on a recording making racially charged comments about his mistress socializing with African Americans during Clippers games. In the ensuing firestorm, the NBA took the unprecedented step of compelling the Sterling family to sell the franchise. Sterling initially brought legal action against the NBA and others to halt the sale, but he eventually relented and authorized the sale of the franchise to Microsoft executive Steve Ballmer for $2 billion.

I was reluctant to include a profile of Donald Sterling in this book, based on his history of racism and highly questionable ethics. (Many examples of poor behavior predated the recording that resulted in his demise.) I ultimately decided to include his profile in hopes that it would serve as a cautionary tale: achieving massive financial success in business does not excuse reprehensible behavior. It is more than disappointing that someone with Sterling's background—the son of immigrants who faced discrimination himself during his early professional career—could treat others with such disrespect. Nevertheless, in the end, justice was served.

LEWIS KATZ—KINNEY PARKING SYSTEMS
(NEW JERSEY NETS)

Lewis Katz never forgot his roots as a kid from the streets of Camden, New Jersey. He was born in 1942, and lost his father when he was just a year old. His mother worked hard to provide for the family, and Lewis did his part to help while he set out on his path to success. He graduated from Temple University in 1963 and went on to attend law school at Dickinson College (now part of the Pennsylvania State University system), earning his JD in 1966 and graduating first in his class.

Katz went on to found the law firm Katz, Ettin & Levine and served as outside general counsel to the South Jersey Port Corporation and the New Jersey Expressway Authority. Notwithstanding his forays into law, Katz was destined to make his name in the business world. He made his fortune through shrewd investments in parking, banking, outdoor advertising, and real estate. Katz was a turnaround man, and in the case of Kinney Parking and his banking interests, he acquired assets that were out of favor and, applying his gritty work ethic and street smarts, turned those assets into immensely profitable gems. He also partnered with another street-smart dealmaker from South Philadelphia named Tom Glenn to build a profitable business through his company Interstate Outdoor Advertising.

Katz was deeply devoted to his family, and eventually brought his son, Drew, into the business. Drew, who also attended law school, is responsible for growing the family's assets today. Katz branched out into the world of sports through his ownership of the New Jersey Nets and as a member of the investment group Puck Holdings, which owned the New Jersey Devils. Applying his turnaround skill to a troubled franchise, Katz helped the Nets reach the NBA finals in the 2002–2003 season. A year later, he sold the team for more than twice what the investment group paid for the franchise.

Lewis Katz is yet another example of an Alpha who perfectly illustrates the American Dream. He grew up extremely poor in the tough, gritty city of

Camden, New Jersey. Determined to pull himself out of poverty, he latched onto the practice of law as a way out. With one foot in his law practice in the leafy suburbs of Cherry Hill, New Jersey, Katz leveraged all his legal knowledge and combined it with his street smarts to build a diversified business empire. As a testament to Lewis Katz and his ability to build a high-quality team of people around him (including his talented son Drew and former partner, Glenn), the Katz business continues to thrive many years after his tragic death in a plane accident in Massachusetts.   * * *

CHAPTER NINE

The New School

Throughout the book thus far, most of the Alphas we have profiled were either members of the greatest generation, many of whom served in World War II, or were born in the years following World War II and are part of the baby boomer generation. This is not surprising, given that in almost all these cases, they spent twenty years or more building their business interests before reaching Alpha status. In this chapter, however, we profile five members of a "New School" of Alphas, who graduated from law school in the late 1980s or early 1990s and have reached Alpha status seemingly overnight.

While each of these men participated, in one way or another, in the digital boom of the last twenty years, one should resist the urge to chalk their success up to simply being in the right place at the right time. Rather, as you will see, in each case they applied the very same Alpha Characteristics as all the other Alphas on their respective paths to success. In the case of the New School Alphas, they just happened to do so during a period of American business history where millionaires (and in some cases, billionaires) have been minted at a blinding pace.

* * *

PETER THIEL—PAYPAL, PALANTIR, FACEBOOK (AND MORE)

Peter Thiel was born in Frankfurt, Germany. When he was still very young, his family immigrated to the United States. The family moved around at first, eventually settling in California in 1977 when Thiel was ten years old. He was a brilliant student, an avid chess player, and as he reached his teenage years, was drawn to libertarian and conservative ideology.

He earned his undergraduate degree in Philosophy in 1989, and his law degree in 1992, each from Stanford University. After graduating from law school, Thiel faced the disappointment of being turned down for a clerkship with the United States Supreme Court. Nevertheless, he accepted a prestigious clerkship with Judge J.L. Edmondson on the 11th Circuit Court of Appeals. After his clerkship, Thiel embarked on a winding path that would eventually lead to his escape from the law. He joined the prestigious firm Sullivan & Cromwell in New York, where he practiced securities law. After less than a year, however, he left, citing the "lack of transcendental value" of his work. From there, Thiel bounced around, spending time as a speech writer for then-US Secretary of Education William Bennett and as a derivatives trader for Credit Suisse.

In 1996, with $1 million in capital that he scraped together from friends and family, Thiel launched the eponymous Thiel Capital Management, which was a venture capital fund focused on making investments in the emerging dot-com market. Thiel had some winners and losers, but everything changed when he backed a company called Confinity and an entrepreneur named Max Levchin, himself an immigrant and a brilliant computer scientist from the University of Illinois.

In 1999, Thiel and Levchin pivoted with the realization that Confinity's cryptographic technology could be used to facilitate the rapidly growing demand for seamless online payments. The result was a company called PayPal, which Thiel, Levchin, and their team scaled and took public in 2002. Later that year, the company was acquired by eBay for $1.5 billion, and Thiel's stake alone was worth more than $50 million.

From that point in 2002, Thiel's run (which is still going) has been legendary. Thiel was an early investor in companies like Facebook (its first outside investor), Yelp, and LinkedIn, among many others. He is also a co-founder of the mysterious software and data analytics firm Palantir. As an example of his massive success as a venture capital investor, the 10.2 percent stake in Facebook he acquired in 2004 for an investment of $500,000 was worth more than $1 billion when he sold it just *eight years later* in 2012.

Peter Thiel is fiercely independent, contrarian, and willing to risk capital on fledgling companies that have the chance to significantly alter the manner in which we interact with the world around us. His escape from the law was swift and deliberate, but his road to massive success in business was marked with seemingly incongruous stops along the way (i.e., as a speech writer and derivatives trader) that added to the diversity of his experience. Although Thiel's fortune has grown to more than $2 billion, it is fair to say that he is motivated by things much deeper than money. One needs to look no further than his libertarian/conservative ideology, or to his support of certain philanthropic initiatives (through, for example, the Thiel Fellowship and the Thiel Foundation), to conclude that Thiel is primarily driven by maximizing his personal freedom and making his mark in history.

TODD WAGNER—BROADCAST.COM

Todd Wagner may not be a name you recognize, but this native of Gary, Indiana and former lawyer/CPA is a billionaire. While you may have never heard of Wagner, you almost certainly know his former partner—fellow Indiana University alum Mark Cuban.

After graduating from IU in 1983, Wagner earned a law degree from the University of Virginia and then moved to Dallas, Texas, where he joined the law firm Akin, Gump, Strauss, Hauer & Feld. Wagner eventually moved on to a smaller firm called Hopkins & Sutter, where he became a partner and practiced corporate law. By all measures, he had achieved success as a lawyer. He was earning a great living and practicing law in a dynamic city. Yet, by his own admission, he was miserable. He eventually discovered that it wasn't the law firm, or the area of law in which he practiced, or the city in which he was practicing; rather, he just wasn't cut out for the practice of law.

Desperate for help, Wagner enrolled in a course (which was more like a support group) for disgruntled lawyers called "Running from the Law." The group was led by Dr. Helen Harkness, a professor at Southern Methodist University, who realized that many lawyers were struggling to find balance in the profession. With the support and urging of Dr. Harkness, Wagner decided to make the escape from "successful" law firm partner to entrepreneur.

Unlike the reaction Sam Zell received when he broke the news to his firm, when Wagner informed the senior partner at Hopkins & Sutter that he was going to resign, the partner told him he was crazy and that he would never make it in business. Nevertheless, Wagner was certain his misery would only deepen if he continued to practice law, and this outweighed his fear of the unknown. So, in 1995, he joined up with Cuban and the duo took over a company called AudioNet, which had been founded by an entrepreneur named Chris Jaeb. Over the next four years, Cuban and Wagner transformed AudioNet (later renamed Broadcast.com) from a sports-focused internet broadcast company into a corporate and commercial internet radio company. The team took Broadcast.com public in 1998 and later sold the company to Yahoo! in 1999 (just before the dot-com bubble burst) for more than $5 billion.

Todd Wagner did not set out to become a billionaire. Rather, he simply sought to use his talents in a way that was more aligned with his values and a lifestyle that would bring him more joy. Wagner certainly benefited from timing, but he left the practice of law without a clear path to riches. After achieving a fantastic financial outcome, Wagner has continued to stay involved in other entrepreneurial endeavors, but has also leveraged his success to support several successful entertainment ventures and many philanthropic causes.

ERIC LEFKOFSKY AND BRAD KEYWELL—STARBELLY, GROUPON (AND OTHERS)

Eric Lefkofsky was born in Detroit, Michigan in 1969, and raised in Southfield, Michigan, the son of a structural engineer and a school teacher. He attended the University of Michigan, where he earned his undergraduate degree in 1991. He also launched his entrepreneurial journey in college, putting together a business selling carpet to earn extra money. Lefkofsky stayed at the University of Michigan and earned his law degree in 1993, but by then had already decided to make his escape into business.

During law school, Lefkofsky befriended Brad Keywell, who was also a Michigan native who earned both his undergraduate and law degrees from the University of Michigan. The two newly minted lawyers eschewed the practice of law. With $1 million raised from family and friends, they acquired a company called Brandon Apparel, which sold athletic clothing. As the duo worked to scale their apparel business, a new world of online commerce was exploding.

Between 1996 and 2006, Lefkofsky, Keywell, and other partners were involved with the founding of several internet startup companies, with varying degrees of success. They were being dogged by creditors and lawsuits stemming from their failed venture with Brandon Apparel. Then, in 2000, they hit pay dirt when they sold an e-commerce company called Starbelly.com, which sold promotional merchandise over the internet, to Ha-Lo Industries for $240 million.

Following the sale of Starbelly, Lefkofsky and Keywell pursued other interests and partnered in co-founding several other businesses, a few of which have gone public and added to their already impressive success. In 2007, they joined forces with Andrew Mason and co-founded ThePoint.com, an online collective action company that was eventually renamed Groupon. Groupon raised millions of dollars in capital and went public in 2011. At the time, it was the largest IPO involving a web-based company since Google went public in 2004. Lefkofsky has since served Groupon in a variety of capacities, including as CEO from 2013 to 2015, and has remained a member of the board. Groupon's success earned Lefkofsky and Keywell hundreds of millions of dollars, and both of them have since made The Giving Pledge.

The path followed by Lefkofsky and Keywell may be of particular interest to those considering law school, as well as those currently attending law school. First, their partnership illustrates the importance of developing relationships with likeminded people during one's formative years of education. While those relationships might not result in professional partnerships, it is entirely possible that one could meet their "business soul mate," and find a partner to share the experience of pursuing success through entrepreneurship. It is also important to note the key takeaway—that students should observe market trends and be willing to pursue unique opportunities in rising markets. Depending on when one is reading this book, that may be cybersecurity, artificial intelligence, deep learning, or markets that have yet to be created. The bottom line is, successful escapes from the practice of law (even by those who never start practicing in the first place) often start with leveraging one's network and then stepping into active, rapidly growing markets, seeking ways to add value.

CHRIS SACCA—LOWERCASE CAPITAL

Chris Sacca is another name that you may recognize if you're plugged in to Silicon Valley or a fan of the hit show *Shark Tank*. Today, Sacca is the founder and a partner with Lowercase Capital, a venture capital firm based on the West Coast. But not long ago, he embarked on a legal career that would eventually lead him to early-stage investments in Twitter, Uber, and Instagram. Sacca's path has been anything but linear.

Sacca was born in Lockport, New York in 1975 and was raised there by his father, who practiced law, and his mother, who was a professor at SUNY Buffalo. By all indications, Sacca was a precocious and inquisitive child and was fortunate to be encouraged to understand the true value of learning and hard work.

Sacca went on to attend the School of Foreign Service at Georgetown University, where he earned his B.A. in 1997, and later enrolled in the Georgetown University Law Center, where he graduated *cum laude* in 2000. Sacca graduated at the height of the internet craze and traveled west to be part of the action. He landed at Fenwick & West, where he focused on venture capital, M&A, and licensing transactions for technology clients. A little more than a year into his practice, however, he was a victim of the massive layoffs that followed the epic burst of the internet bubble.

Opportunities for lawyers, especially those with limited experience, were slim in the immediate aftermath of the bubble burst, and so Sacca spent the next few years doing freelance work and networking in the Valley. Due in large part to his tireless efforts to meet and help people in his business network, Sacca landed at a company called Speedera Networks. Once there, he leveraged his experience to eventually be hired as Corporate Counsel at Google, where he worked directly with the company's chief legal officer, David Drummond.

Once inside Google, Sacca found his stride in business. His first project as Corporate Counsel was to locate data space around the world and negotiate agreements to lock up data storage capacity for Google. Sacca produced outstanding results and leveraged his early success into another role with Google, as Head of Special Initiatives. In that role, he continued to hone his skills as dealmaker, eventually moving into broader M&A transactions and a business development role with Google. In December 2007, less than ten years after graduating from law school, Sacca left Google (with his stock fully vested) and took the leap into the world of angel investing.

Through Lowercase Capital, Sacca made up for his lack of access to significant amounts of capital with his direct, hands-on involvement with the companies in which he invested. All the years of networking, hard work, and adding value in the marketplace paid off, and Sacca landed opportunities to invest in and advise companies like Twitter, Uber, and Instagram, among others, well before their first institutional rounds of financing.

Today, Sacca conducts business from his mountain retreat in Truckee, California. He is the happily married father of three, and is actively involved in political and charitable causes. He is vocal on Twitter and one of the most respected voices in the Valley. Sacca overcame adversity early in his legal career, and was willing to play the long game, methodically building his network and seeking to add value for others along the way. As importantly, the diversity of his experience at Fenwick, Speedera, and Google made him extremely valuable to the budding startups he would eventually support and advise on their way to explosive growth.

* * *

The New School of Alphas profiled in this chapter offers a glimpse into the future of the escape from law into business. While there will remain opportunities in traditional industries, private equity, hedge fund investing, and energy, there are now exciting new opportunities for lawyers to transition into emerging technologies and other twenty-first-century businesses. While at first blush, one might conclude that lawyers and technology don't mix, for companies to find profitable applications for these technologies, they must have leaders who can analyze, organize, negotiate, execute, and communicate the tremendous value of those technologies to others who often lack deep technological understanding themselves. These are skills that lawyers develop through the rigors of education and practice, and can therefore bring to the market to add value.

This chapter also demonstrates that the rise from lawyer to Alpha is not something reserved for a bygone era. Rather, opportunities abound today and will continue into the future for lawyers who are willing to draw on their Alpha Characteristics to find their unique path to entrepreneurship.

CHAPTER TEN

Passion

The Alphas profiled thus far have earned hundreds of millions, if not billions, of dollars in their chosen fields. Many have branched out into new markets, often in areas that reflect their personal passions, applying their skills to areas that are more purely based on avocational interests (such as professional sports, art, restaurants, or other businesses). Perhaps after reading the previous chapters, some of you remain skeptical that there is an escape for you. Or, perhaps you lack an interest in the fields of business we have explored thus far.

In this chapter, we profile ten individuals who have successfully transitioned from the practice of law and moved into areas of business closely aligned with their personal interests. My hope with this chapter is that any remaining skeptics will see that the escape can be equally successful and rewarding when pursuing a unique path based on one's passion. While some of the individuals profiled in this chapter are extremely wealthy, each of them has pursued their chosen path based on sincere passion for subjects like entertainment, sports, negotiation, publishing, food, and wine, and the financial success that followed was just an added (albeit substantial) bonus.

* * *

LEON CHARNEY—L.H. CHARNEY & ASSOCIATES

Leon Charney was a colorful character who grew up in a poor Jewish family in New Jersey. He was born in Bayonne, New Jersey in 1938, where he attended Jewish day schools. He went on to attend Yeshiva University, where he earned money to pay for his education by singing in his synagogue.

Charney earned his undergraduate degree from Yeshiva in 1960, and then earned his law degree from Brooklyn Law School in 1964. With the hubris of a newly minted law school graduate, Charney took all the money he could scrape together—$200—and started his own law firm. Eventually, through sheer determination and a little luck, Charney developed a practice representing sports figures and entertainers, including Sammy Davis, Jr. and Jackie Mason.

For many, building a law practice representing athletes, musicians, and movie stars would be a dream come true. But Charney was a man of many interests. At thirty-six, he became an advisor to Vance Hartke, a United States senator and vocal opponent of the Vietnam War. For the next six years, Charney served Hartke as his special counsel, and then later served as an informal advisor to President Jimmy Carter with respect to the Camp David Accords between Israel and Egypt.

In 1980, while in his early forties, Charney made his first real estate investment, acquiring a property at One Times Square. Over the next thirty-plus years, Charney built an impressive portfolio of prime real estate assets and, in the process, made himself a billionaire.

If this were the end of the story, Charney would have been included in Chapter 4, where his rags-to-riches story would have fit well with the other real estate moguls profiled in that chapter. But, as noted above, Charney was a man of many interests and talents. While he made his fortune in real estate, he made his mark on the world as an author and political pundit, focused on foreign affairs, Judaism, social issues, and popular culture. Charney hosted a nationally syndicated talk show (*The Charney Report*) and authored four books, his last being *The Mystery of the Kaddish: Its Profound Influence on Judaism*, published in 2006.

When one sums up Leon Charney's life in a sentence or two, it does not sound believable. Here was a poor boy from Bayonne, New Jersey, who became a husband, father, cantor, attorney, real estate tycoon, author, political pundit, and philanthropist. After leaving his boyhood home in New Jersey, his travels took him from Manhattan to Tel Aviv and beyond. Although he died in 2016 at the age of seventy-seven, his life and work live on through his books and the impact he made on so many lives.

MORT ZUCKERMAN—REAL ESTATE & PUBLISHING

Mort Zuckerman was born in Montreal, Canada in 1937, where his parents Abraham and Esther owned a small tobacco and candy shop. His grandfather was an Orthodox Rabbi, and Zuckerman was raised in a very devout and tight-knit family. He was extremely bright and entered McGill University when he was just sixteen years old, earning his undergraduate and law degrees, although he did not sit for the bar in Canada.

In 1961, Zuckerman came to America, where he earned his MBA from the University of Pennsylvania with honors. In 1962, Zuckerman moved on to Harvard University, where he supplemented his law degree from McGill with an LLM from Harvard Law School. He then accepted a teaching position at Harvard Business School.

While he was teaching at Harvard, Zuckerman earned a position with Cabot, Cabot & Forbes, where he learned the real estate business and eventually rose to the role of senior vice president and chief financial officer. As with Leon Charney, while Zuckerman was building wealth in real estate, he ventured into a new field that sparked his passions for political punditry and publishing. At various points over the last thirty years or so, Zuckerman has been the owner and publisher of such magazines as *The Atlantic Monthly*, *Fast Company*, and *U.S. News & World Report*. In addition, Zuckerman is a frequent editorialist and commentator on world affairs, appearing in the pages of his publishing properties, as well as on *The McLaughlin Report*, and among the talking heads on MSNBC.

Zuckerman's path demonstrates the value of remaining open to various ways to earn a living, while also finding outlets for one's passions. Although

Zuckerman never practiced law, his deep respect for education (no doubt instilled in him by his parents and his grandfather) led him to pursue knowledge in multiple disciplines, which he then brought to bear when he moved into real estate and publishing.

JIM CRAMER—HEDGE FUNDS, AUTHOR, TELEVISION PERSONALITY

If you have ever tuned in to CNBC during the opening bell, or in the early evening for the show *Mad Money*, you have probably seen a man with rolled-up shirt sleeves and an animated disposition, slapping buttons and holding forth on stocks in a variety of industries. If so, then you are familiar with Jim Cramer. Cramer was born outside of Philadelphia, in Wyndmoor, PA in 1955. His mother was an artist, while his father owned a company called International Packaging Products, selling wrapping paper, boxes and bags to retailers.

Jim Cramer is a "Philly guy" through and through. One of his first jobs was selling ice cream at the old Veteran's Stadium during Philadelphia Phillies baseball games in the summer. In the late 1970s, Cramer left Philadelphia for Boston, where he earned his undergraduate degree from Harvard University in 1977 and became Editor-in-Chief of *The Harvard Crimson*. Between college and law school, Cramer pursued a career in journalism, working for papers in Florida and California. He covered the Ted Bundy serial murder case, among other stories including sports and politics. Later, Cramer moved from California to New York, where he helped launch *The American Lawyer* magazine.

As with all the people profiled in this chapter, Cramer followed a winding path into and out of the law and seems to have enjoyed every minute of it. He returned to Harvard in 1981 and earned his law degree in 1984. While he was in law school, he worked as a research assistant to Alan Dershowitz during his defense of Claus von Bulow, and also started trading stocks on the side.

While Cramer performed well in law school, he had greater success trading stocks, which led him to accept a role with Goldman Sachs upon graduation. In 1987, just three years removed from law school, he left Goldman and founded his own hedge fund called Cramer & Co. (later renamed Cramer, Berkowitz & Co.). From 1988 to 2000 (when Cramer left the fund), he produced annual returns of more than 20 percent per year, and routinely personally earned over $10 million a year.

As with any good polymath, Cramer was not satisfied doing just one thing. And so, in addition to managing the fund, he also served as editor-at-large for *SmartMoney* magazine. Then, in 1996, he launched The Street, Inc. (formerly known as TheStreet.com, Inc.), a financial news and services site where Cramer indulged his passion for writing and connecting with people on the subject of the stock market.

Beginning in the late '90s, Cramer also became a recurring guest on CNBC. His first crack at his own show came with economist Larry Kudlow. *Kudlow & Cramer* was styled as a business and political commentary program and ran for three years. Cramer's dynamic, irreverent, and passionate persona was perfect for CNBC, as he livened up what had been dry, cookie-cutter programming before his arrival at the network. In 2005, after *Kudlow & Cramer* wound up, he launched *Mad Money*, which is currently one of the longest-running business and finance shows in American history. Cramer has published several books on investing, as well as his underrated memoir called *Confessions of a Street Addict*, through which he has developed a loyal following of viewers and readers who seemingly devour all the content he can produce.

Jim Cramer's success as a hedge fund trader produced fabulous wealth that has enabled him to spend almost twenty years sharing everything he has learned with others. If one steps back for a moment, however, it is easy to see how Cramer's background, coupled with his varied experiences, fit together into a cohesive story. First, Cramer was raised in a loving family, where his father was an entrepreneur and his mother was an artist, thus instilling in Jim both a love for business and a passion for creative pursuits. Cramer then combined his natural intelligence with his dogged work ethic to earn admission to Harvard University, where he developed a passion for storytelling (i.e., journalism) and rose to become Editor-in-Chief of the fabled campus newspaper, the *Harvard Crimson*. He took his time and lived simply while he followed stories of national importance, and then gradually made his way back to Harvard to pursue his law degree.

It is not surprising that Cramer skipped the practice of law altogether and went directly into trading stocks, given that he was trading and earning fantastic returns while he was a student. Perhaps drawing on his father's example of entrepreneurial risk, Cramer then left Goldman Sachs after only a few years and set up his own shop. To his credit, while Cramer could still be running a fund today and would possibly be much wealthier than he already is, he stepped away from the table, collected his winnings, and set off to do something different.

There are many lessons to be learned from Jim Cramer's journey, but there are two that warrant special attention. First, for those who are considering or currently attending law school, his story demonstrates the importance of taking one's time. Cramer could have gone directly from his undergraduate studies to law school, but he took several years to pursue his passion for journalism. While living simply and moving around, chasing stories that piqued his interest, he developed skills that would become extremely valuable much later in life. Second, Cramer's life perfectly illustrates the important discipline of knowing when to walk away. Too many people live what author Tim Ferriss calls a "deferred life plan," waiting for an undefined point in the future to do many of the things they want to. Cramer has been guided by a clear vision of his ideal life. When he earned enough money to support the lifestyle he wanted to live, he turned his attention to writing and television, where he has shared his expertise with millions of people.

RON SHAPIRO—SPORTS AGENT AND AUTHOR

Ron Shapiro has built a varied and fascinating career, and is perhaps one of the few people profiled in this book who has remained closest to his legal roots throughout his career. Shapiro was born in Philadelphia, Pennsylvania in 1943, and raised in the suburb of Cheltenham. He stayed in the Philadelphia area for college and graduated from Haverford College, a well-regarded private liberal arts school, in 1964. Shapiro then went on to Harvard University, where he earned his law degree in 1967.

After graduating from law school, Shapiro moved to Baltimore, Maryland, where he worked in private practice and then served as the State Securities

Commissioner from 1972 to 1974. While he was serving as securities commissioner, Shapiro took the entrepreneurial step of starting his own law firm, which was called Shapiro, Sher, Guinot & Sandler. Through a series of seemingly unconnected events, Shapiro had the opportunity to do some work for Brooks Robinson, a local legend who played baseball for the Baltimore Orioles. Shapiro leveraged that one engagement into an entirely new career.

In 1976, Shapiro founded Shapiro, Robinson & Associates, a sports management firm that has represented such athletes as Cal Ripkin, Jr., Jim Palmer, Kirby Puckett, Eddie Murray and Joe Mauer. Shapiro helped Mauer negotiate what was, at the time, one of the most lucrative contracts in baseball history, while at the same time ensuring that the Minnesota Twins held onto their superstar (a Win-win deal, which is Shapiro's trademark approach, in which both sides win, but his client gets the "capital W"). Based on his success in baseball, Shapiro has gained experience in other professional sports. In those engagements, he has worked the other side of the table as an advisor to the owner of the Baltimore Ravens of the NFL, and to the general managers of the Oklahoma Thunder, the Orlando Magic, and the San Antonio Spurs of the NBA.

While Shapiro has built a fantastic business negotiating deals in professional sports, his great passion has been to teach his unique brand of negotiation to others in a variety of businesses and nonprofit environments. In 1995, he launched the Shapiro Negotiations Institute, through which he works with individuals and corporations to teach people the value of diligent preparation and his Win-win approach to negotiation. In addition to his consulting work, Shapiro is the author of several books on negotiation, which I believe are among the best (if not the best) on the subject (at least for those who prefer to build lasting relationships and design creative solutions to complex problems, as opposed to the short-sighted method of zero-sum negotiation).

Many of us would love nothing more than to build a practice representing athletes, sports teams, and other entertainers. What is interesting about Shapiro, however, is that he never set out to do that. Rather, he was a business lawyer running his own law firm when he just happened to have the opportunity to help Brooks Robinson with a business deal. Shapiro added so much value and impressed Robinson so much that it opened an entire world of opportunity. Had Shapiro gone into that engagement hoping or expecting to build an entire practice around representing athletes, he most likely would have failed because his insincerity would have been obvious. Instead, he genuinely sought a creative solution to his client's problem, and the reward for the value he delivered was a future of remarkable opportunities.

DONALD DELL—PROSERV

Unless you are an avid tennis player or a student of the history of the game, you have likely never heard the name Donald Dell. One of many things that make Dell's story unique among his peers in this book is that he is the sole professional athlete turned lawyer turned sports agent that we profile. What he shares with other Alphas, and particularly those in this chapter, is that he leveraged his innate talent and applied his Alpha Characteristics of diligence and tolerance for risk to achieve notable success in a very competitive field.

Donald Dell was born in Savannah, Georgia in 1938, where he developed a passion for tennis at a young age and earned a position on the men's tennis team at Yale University. He earned his undergraduate degree from Yale in 1960, and was talented enough to play on the professional circuit thereafter. He also had a deep desire to attend law school. Although it was extremely difficult to balance, he attended the University of Virginia School of Law while continuing to play tennis professionally, including participation on the United States Davis Cup team.

Upon graduating from law school in 1964, Dell accepted a position with the Washington, D.C. firm of Hogan & Hartson. After the excitement of playing tennis internationally, becoming an office-bound associate, even at a firm as well-regarded as Hogan & Harston, was unbearable. Dell left the firm after only eighteen months. While he kept one foot in the tennis world, he also pursued other professional opportunities. Remaining in Washington, D.C., Dell went to work for Sargent Shriver, who was tackling President Lyndon Johnson's War on Poverty through the newly created Office of Economic Opportunity. Initially, Dell's responsibilities focused on research and writing.

But eventually, he was traveling the world with Shriver, where he sat in on meetings with global leaders.

By 1968, just four years out of law school, the siren song of tennis harkened, and Dell rejoined the men's US Davis Cup Team, this time as team captain. Under his leadership, the team went undefeated and Dell developed a reputation as a strong advocate for professional tennis. At the time, tennis was on the cusp of entering its "golden age," filled with dynamic personalities like Arthur Ashe, Jimmy Conners, Stan Smith, John McEnroe, Ivan Lendl, Bjorn Borg, Yannick Noah, and many others, which included some of the most compelling rivalries in all of sports. Dell was uniquely positioned to professionalize the business side of tennis, and he seized the opportunity.

Initially, Dell approached his old firm (Hogan & Hartson) about developing a sports law practice within the firm. Hogan & Harston was supportive and offered him office space and a dedicated team of lawyers to support the practice, but Dell reconsidered when thinking through the fact that the practice would ultimately belong to Hogan & Hartson, rather than himself. Dell had a deep desire to build something of his own, and so he ultimately decided to start his own law firm along with a few friends and former colleagues from Hogan. After practicing law for a few years, Dell formed a separate sports management firm called Professional Services, Inc. (ProServ), with a specific focus on professional tennis. Over the years, Dell represented some of the biggest names in the game, including Ashe, Conners, Smith, and Lendl. His firm eventually branched out to represent athletes in other sports, including Patrick Ewing and Michael Jordan. Beyond representing athletes, Dell also developed a deep expertise negotiating endorsement contracts and other high-value arrangements with companies like Adidas and Nike. At its peak, before Dell sold ProServ in 1999, it represented more than 200 athletes and was an early pioneer of negotiating naming rights for such properties as FedEx Field, Phillips Arena, and Staples Center.

Even after selling his firm, Dell remained active in both tennis and deal making. In 2009, he released a book called *Never Make the First Offer (Except When You Should): Wisdom from a Master Dealmaker*. In it, he provides an inside look at some of the most interesting deals he negotiated throughout his career and the negotiating principles that can be drawn from his experience. The life of Donald Dell is an example of the remarkable success (and fun!) one can achieve when passion meets business.

LARRY FLAX & RICK ROSENFIELD— CALIFORNIA PIZZA KITCHEN

Business partnerships can be complicated. When two or more lawyers come together to form a firm, the relationships can be strained if one partner brings in more business than the other, or another partner is doing more of the heavy lifting. Often, however, partnerships can work beautifully, with each party bringing something unique to the table that is valued by the others. While such successful partnerships are common, it is quite rare to see one that spans multiple industries and lasts for more than forty years.

Larry Flax and Rick Rosenfield are two partners who defied the odds and built not only a very successful law firm, but also a nationally recognized restaurant chain. Larry Flax was born in 1944 and earned his B.A. from the University of Washington, and then his law degree from the University of Southern California a few years later. Rick Rosenfield is three years younger than Flax, and graduated from DePaul University School of Law. The two men met when they were both working as Assistant United States Attorneys in Los Angeles, California.

In 1971, Flax convinced Rosenfield to leave the US Attorney's office and go into private practice. Just one year later, the men focused on criminal defense work in their own firm, Flax & Rosenfield. Over the next decade, the men built a highly successful practice. But as with many lawyers, they found little time for anything else. They both loved to cook and wanted to open a restaurant together, but their burgeoning practice always seemed to get in the way. In 1984, they were deeply engaged in a multi-month criminal trial in San Francisco, which took them away from their families and further fueled their desire to do something different.

Later that year, after the trial in San Francisco concluded, they shuttered their law practice and opened a restaurant called California Pizza Kitchen in Beverly Hills. At that time, Rosenfield was married and had a two-and-a-half-year-old daughter, while Flax was dating a woman who lived in Houston, Texas. Nevertheless, they embraced the risk, scraped together $225,000 between the two of them, and raised another $275,000 from friends and family. They opened their first restaurant in 1985 at a total cost of $500,000. Just seven years later, they had twenty-five company-owned California Pizza Kitchen restaurants and were generating more than $55 million in annual revenue. By 2011, not quite thirty years after escaping the practice of law, that number had grown to more than 300 restaurants in sixteen different countries, and the partners sold the business to a private equity firm for $470 million.

The story of Flax and Rosenfield further supports the concept of having the courage to know when to step away. Given their personal situations, it would have been easy for Rosenfield and Flax to come up with a list of reasons why shutting down a profitable law practice (which they even enjoyed, to a certain extent) in favor of starting a pizza restaurant was a terrible idea. Had their sole, or even primary, motivation been to make a lot of money, they almost certainly would not have made the move. But, after working themselves to exhaustion on a complex criminal trial, they realized that there would never be a "right time" to pursue their passion and open a restaurant. They were willing to play the long game, and almost thirty years later, they earned a massive financial reward for a risk they took in 1984. I am willing to bet, however, that if you asked them whether they would make the same decision knowing they would only end up with a few restaurants and modest financial returns, they would do it all again (only maybe sooner).

JESS STONESTREET JACKSON, JR.— JACKSON FAMILY WINES

Jess Jackson is an Alpha who loved practicing law, but reached a point in his life where he was looking for some excitement and found it in the form of grapes. Jackson was born in San Francisco, California in 1930 and grew up during the Great Depression. He learned the value of a strong work ethic from an early age as he held several different jobs throughout adolescence so that he could contribute to his family's needs.

Jackson attended the University of California, where he earned both his undergraduate and law degrees. Upon his graduation from law school in 1951, he went into private practice and a few years later took his first entrepreneurial step and formed his own law firm where he focused on real estate, land use, and property rights cases. His practice was very successful, and during his career, he argued several cases before the United States Supreme Court. He was also well-regarded by his fellow attorneys, and thus became one of the founding members of the California Trial Lawyers Association.

In 1974, at the age of forty-four, and after more than twenty years running his law firm, Jackson and his then-wife Jane Kendall Jackson took a risk and acquired an eighty-acre parcel of land in Lakeport, California with the goal of starting a family vineyard. Jackson's passion for wine resulted in the development of several varietals that bridged the gap between ultra-premium and super-cheap wines, and thereby offered consumers a reliable and fairly priced bottle of quality wine.

By the time of his death in 2011 at the age of eighty-one, Jackson had a net worth of nearly $2 billion. In just one generation, he went from growing up in the depths of the Great Depression to being an internationally known vintner and creating wealth that will last for generations. But, as with the others profiled in this chapter, one could reasonably conclude that if he had simply lived the rest of his days on that eighty-acre orchard and produced only a few cases of wine a year to be shared with family and friends, he would have been just as happy. Jackson knew poverty and worked hard to avoid it the rest of his days. But what drove his success was a love of the process, not a pot of gold at the end of the vineyard.

NINA AND TIM ZAGAT—THE ZAGAT RESTAURANT SURVEYS

Continuing the theme of food and wine, Nina and Tim Zagat have perhaps the most romantic (or maybe the only romantic) business story profiled in this book. The couple met when they were both students at Yale University School of Law, graduating in 1966. They were married during law school and together moved to New York City, where they each practiced corporate law with different Wall Street firms.

After a few years in New York, Nina and Tim each accepted separate opportunities to practice law in Paris—Nina with Shearman & Sterling, and Tim with the firm Hughes Hubbard & Reed. While in Paris, the couple indulged their love of fine food and casually compiled a list of their favorite restaurants, noting what they liked and didn't like along the way. This led to the idea of creating a restaurant guide and review publication to provide others like them with deeper insights into the best restaurants in certain cities.

Once back in New York, they compiled reviews and ratings for restaurants throughout Manhattan and published their first *Zagat* restaurant guide in 1982, which they sold in local bookstores. By 1984, the *Zagat* guide became a well-regarded fine dining resource and was selling more than 40,000 copies per year. What started as a fun hobby had become a profitable business, and the Zagats each left their respective practices to devote all their focus to this growing enterprise. Over the next thirty years, the *Zagat* guide grew to include more restaurants in many other cities, and their name became synonymous with restaurant reviews. In 2011, the Zagats sold the company to Google for more than $150 million.

Nina and Tim Zagat were Yale-educated lawyers who reached the pinnacle of the profession—not just working for white-shoe law firms, but having the opportunity to practice internationally. Yet, they took something that was a shared passion (fine dining) and almost by accident turned it into a scalable business. They both continued to practice law until the success of their "side hustle" required all their time, and only then did they escape the practice of law. The result was a business that combined their passion with their expertise in restaurants and they delivered something of immense value to the market. While they did not set out to create an asset worth more than $100 million, by combining their passion with their intellect and ability to build something of value, the Zagats gave themselves a profitable escape from the law.

* * *

If you were to ask three people whether it makes sense to give up the practice of law to "chase your passion," you would likely get three different answers. One might say that such a move would be irresponsible; it's all well and good to be passionate about something, but giving up a high-six-figure salary to chase one's passion to cook, or write, or coach, or do anything else without any clear means of earning a living would be foolish. Another might tell you that if you do something that energizes you so much that you can spend hours doing it and become so engrossed in the process that you lose track of time, then you will never really "work" another day in your life. As for the financial considerations, if you are good enough at whatever that is, then the money will almost certainly follow. While there is a kernel of truth in each of these viewpoints, there is a third perspective, which is reflected in the lives of the individuals profiled above.

As noted earlier, it would be disingenuous to minimize the importance (and responsibility) of earning a living. Many people who go into the practice of law do not come from wealth, and thus have steep loans that must be repaid. In many circumstances, those people have a spouse and children to whom they have made a commitment to provide (at a minimum) the necessities of food, shelter, and safety. But if priorities are aligned correctly, it is possible to indulge and pursue one's passion while continuing to practice law until the money coming in is sufficient to cover the basics.

Leon Charney built a practice representing entertainers until he was stable enough to branch out into politics and real estate, and only then did he pursue his passion (in his forties) for political commentary and writing. Likewise, Mort Zuckerman started working in real estate while he was still pursuing his advanced degrees, and then taught at Harvard until he could personally invest in real estate. His methodical process of building his real estate portfolio then allowed him to move into publishing, which gave him an outlet for his passion for covering world affairs. Jim Cramer worked in journalism, then leveraged his skill in analyzing and trading public equities to provide a strong financial base, which allowed him to come full circle and pursue his passion for writing and providing insight on the stock market and current affairs.

Ron Shapiro and Donald Dell took different approaches to the business of sports management, but in each case leveraged their legal background to provide excellent service to their clients. At the same time, they had fun mixing their love of sports with their passion for business and negotiation. Larry Flax and Rick Rosenfield, as well as Nina and Tim Zagat, practiced law just long enough to provide the freedom to pursue their respective passions in the restaurant and food business. And Jess Jackson, a widely respected real estate and trial lawyer who argued several cases before the highest court in the land, used an eighty-acre plot of land that he originally bought in his mid-forties because he was in search of something "different" to spawn the creation of a family enterprise that has changed an entire industry.

If you look around, you will find that many people inside and outside the practice of law find ways to turn their respective passions into real, thriving businesses. Not all passions can be converted into a profitable enterprise to replace one's income from practicing law. However, if one is willing to apply creativity, dedication, and hard work, they might be surprised by the niche markets that exist out there (or can be created) and might one day open a hatch to escape the practice of law. As far as jobs go, a successful law practice can be one of the most lucrative from which a person can earn enough cash to pay the bills and gradually save investment capital that can ultimately be used to turn one's passion into a real business.

PART THREE
ESCAPING THE LAW

CHAPTER ELEVEN

Define Success

I f after reading the profiles set forth in this book, your plan is to stand up from your desk, walk through the door of your law firm, and embark on a journey to "somehow" become a billionaire, then you have missed the point. One who walks away from the practice of law with the primary goal of chasing wealth through entrepreneurship is, in my opinion, unlikely to succeed. Any additional money that such a person might somehow earn will not fill the deep yearning that led them to leave the practice of law in the first place.

Rather, it is my sincere hope that by reading the profiles of these fascinating lawyers who successfully transitioned to entrepreneurship, you have unlocked the motivation and confidence to consider a possible escape of your own. Given the variety of life experiences represented through these profiles (from those who grew up poor, to those who faced discrimination, to those who were born into wealth but chose to blaze a trail of their own), you should be able to find at least one Alpha with whom you can relate and model a path forward.

What prevents most lawyers who are unfulfilled (or worse, truly miserable) in the practice of law from making a change is usually a single emotion—fear. This instinct that humans developed as a means of self-preservation has in modern times become an irrational, paralyzing emotion that prevents us from taking chances and achieving that which we are capable of during our brief time on Earth. I think there are three primary fears that keep lawyers from branching out into business: the fear that they will not earn as much money as they earn practicing law; the fear that their peers will think less of them, and they will lose the perceived respect that comes with being a lawyer; and the fear that they will never be able to recover if their attempt to escape the practice of law fails.

Fear is a powerful emotion and one that we should not ignore. It is important, however, to acknowledge our fears, articulate them, and then objectively consider whether they are rational. The Stoic philosopher Seneca, who earned great wealth in his day as an advisor to Nero, urged his students to set aside a certain number of days each month to "practice poverty." In other words, Seneca suggested taking a few days each month to fast or eat only small amounts of food, wear one's worst clothes, step away from the comforts of one's home, and, by doing so, come face to face with the situation he dreads.

What one is likely to discover through this practice of poverty, however, is that the "worst-case" scenario isn't nearly as awful as we fear. This is not intended to minimize the truly devastating condition of intergenerational poverty, but rather to demonstrate that fears of irreparable ruin among those who are highly educated, resourceful, and hardworking are most likely greatly exaggerated. As stated before, and as illustrated in several profiles in this book, given enough time and determination, there are few situations from which one is truly incapable of recovering.

After facing, naming, and disarming the fears that may be holding one back, they are ready to step forward and define their vision of success. When enduring the status quo becomes painful enough, the motivation to change is usually very powerful. It is at this point that one is ready to go through the exercise of creating a version of what business coach and author Cameron Herold refers to as a "Vivid Vision" of one's life.

I invite you to block out an entire, distraction-free day. This is usually best done out of your office and away from any people or things that will draw your attention from this exercise. Engage in the process of writing in narrative, present-tense[2] form your vision of what success will look and feel like for you. Some questions you might answer through your Vivid Vision are:

- Where do I live?
- Who am I with?
- How do I spend my days?
- What industry or industries am I focused on?
- Do I still practice law, and if so, how does that fit with my other entrepreneurial pursuits?
- How have I measured success at milestones along the way?
- How do I dress (for example, casual or formal)? Do I have a style and, if so, what is it? Is it different from the way I dress today?
- What is different about my life? What is the same?
- What do I have more of? What do I have less of?
- What material things do I have that I don't have today? What material things have I given up in order to live the life I designed for myself?
- What contributions (of money, time, resources, etc.) do I make to the communities, institutions, and people who have had a positive influence on my life?

This is just a sample of the questions you might consider as you go through this process. You should feel free to add or subtract as you see fit. While this exercise might seem silly at first, I cannot stress enough the remarkable power of what author and polymath Tim Ferriss calls "Lifestyle Design." We each have the power, through intention and determination, to design and build a life that is uniquely ours. After going through the exercise of writing down in vivid detail the exact picture of the life you truly want to live in the future, you will be amazed how you start to make things happen that support the unique vision of your life that you have designed.

---

2   In other words, even though you are writing about a point in the future (sometimes as many as twenty years hence or more), the narrative should be written as though you are describing your circumstances as they exist at that point in the future. This is a very important part of the exercise, as it provides the framework for one to truly envision themselves living in those circumstances at that point in the future.

I believe this exercise is important for everyone, at any stage in life, but it is an absolutely critical step in the process of planning and executing one's escape from the practice of law. If one lacks a crystal-clear vision of the lifestyle they want to create and the precise areas of business in which they believe they can deliver value in the marketplace, then they will simply be running away from the practice of law without a clear purpose or destination. Only after defining in as much detail as possible their "why" and what success will look like after they escape the practice of law are they ready to develop a detailed escape plan.

CHAPTER TWELVE

Escape Planning

_____

Once you have taken the time to design your ideal lifestyle and define success in vivid detail, you are ready to create a detailed plan of escape from the practice of law. As we think about escape planning, the metaphor of Andy Dufresne's escape from Shawshank Prison in the classic film _Shawshank Redemption_ provides a valuable lesson. Had Andy decided to make his escape and simply run for the fence, it certainly would not have ended well. Instead, Andy spent almost twenty years in Shawshank, plotting, planning, scheming, working, and lining everything up until conditions were aligned for maximum success. Likewise, while one may have the urge to make an immediate escape from the practice of law, they will have a greater likelihood of success if they methodically plan their escape and then take as much time as necessary to execute their plan to perfection.

The precise steps and details of one's escape plan will be unique and will be guided by their individually designed ideal lifestyle and definition of success. Nevertheless, there are certain aspects of escape planning that one should consider in order to maximize success. The following are important considerations and actions that each aspiring escapee should cover in his escape plan:

- *Acknowledge and address deficiencies in physical and spiritual health.* Substance abuse, depression, and generally unhealthy behaviors are unfortunately common among practicing lawyers. It is an extremely stressful profession, and it takes its toll on thousands of lawyers (and their loved ones) every year, sometimes leading to heartbreaking outcomes. Before executing an escape from the practice of law, one should take an inventory of their physical, emotional, and spiritual circumstances and sincerely evaluate whether they would benefit from taking the time to invest in themselves and obtain any required healing before going further. If one is truly miserable and depressed and has started to manifest those feelings through unhealthy behaviors, simply escaping the law and running toward entrepreneurship or anything else will *not* make everything better. For at least a short time, one's stress is likely to increase, and failure to address these serious issues head-on before making an escape from the practice of law will only exacerbate the problem.

- *Read, study and model.* If you have picked up this book, you have taken an important first step toward plotting your escape. One of the best ways to change one's circumstances is to observe others who have done what you want to do and then model your behavior after them to achieve success of your own. Tony Robbins, perhaps the greatest self-help guru of all time, has written several exceptional books that address, among other things, the power of modeling. The profiles in this book provide just surface-level information about lawyers who became successful entrepreneurs. As part of your escape plan, I urge you to engage in much deeper, self-directed study of people (not just lawyers or former lawyers), industries, and companies in the markets that interest you. From that deeper level of studying, you will discover the tools, skills, and attributes that you must acquire or hone to achieve the success you seek.

- *Drill down.* As you engage in the initial level of study discussed above, you will start to identify patterns and specific areas that are of particular interest to you. At that point, it is important to drill down and gain as much knowledge and expertise as you can, so that you may find additional ways to add value in the marketplace beyond what you bring to the table with your legal background. While this could require additional formal training or education, you may be surprised what you can learn on your own if you are simply willing to invest the time.

- *Network and add value without the expectation of immediate personal gain.* One of the most overused, yet barely understood, terms in business is "networking." For those who are naturally introverted, the mere mention of the word invokes fear and loathing. Even for those who are naturally outgoing and genuinely enjoy meeting new people, the well-meaning encouragement to "build your network" rarely comes along with any useful advice for how to do so in a genuine way. There are too many people who take a shotgun approach, handing out their business card to any warm body they happen to encounter and adding contacts on LinkedIn as though it were a game. For those seeking to escape the practice of law, you must be much more thoughtful about how and why you are building your network. The purpose of a truly valuable business network is to create a web of interconnected relationships among people with shared experiences or interests, with the intention of finding ways to add value and truly help as many members of that network as possible. This approach to networking is perfectly illustrated by the words of world-renowned sales coach Zig Ziglar, who said, "You can have everything in life you want, if you will just help enough other people get what they want." Stated differently, the value of your network to you is directly proportional to the number of other people to whom you can add value and help within that network. With that in mind, building a valuable network should focus on the quality of relationships, not the quantity of people in the network. And, perhaps most importantly, you should be prepared to give much more than you receive. If you approach networking as a game to produce immediate benefits for yourself, it will be painfully obvious to others and your efforts will likely be in vain. As entrepreneur and speaker Gary Vaynerchuk advises in his book *Jab, Jab, Jab, Right Hook*, in the modern business environment, it is more important than ever to add value, contribute, and help others (i.e., "jab, jab, jab") before asking for anything from them (i.e., the "right hook").

- *Be the best lawyer you can be.* While a few Alphas did not spend any time practicing law, most spent at least a few years in practice, and many spent a decade or more during which they developed valuable domain expertise that served them well in their entrepreneurial pursuits. If you are currently practicing law, or are in law school and expect to spend some time practicing before you make your escape, you should devote yourself to becoming the best lawyer you can be and focus on areas of practice that will give you an edge in business. As important as the expertise will be to you, the impression you leave with the attorneys with whom you work is just as essential. One should never burn a bridge if it is avoidable. As you may recall, even though Sam Zell spent less than a month practicing law, he made such a favorable impression on the senior lawyer with whom he worked that the law firm allowed him to work out of its office and paid him referral fees for driving business to the firm. This provided Zell with cash and the platform he needed as he was getting his real estate business off the ground.

- *Be disciplined regarding personal finance.* One of the most common excuses lawyers use for being unable to escape the practice of law is that they cannot "afford" to make the move. In other words, between student loans and the lifestyle to which they (and perhaps their spouse and children) have become accustomed, they cannot walk away from the practice of law to pursue entrepreneurship when they might make less money, even if it is only for a relatively short time. Personal finance is perhaps one of the most critical considerations in developing an escape plan, and it requires humility and the ability to be completely honest with oneself. One must ask whether they (and, if they are married, their spouse) are willing to make the necessary sacrifices to move from law into entrepreneurship. Many lawyers live well above their means to portray a certain image to those around them, and they lack the discipline and humility to scale back their lifestyle to build up the savings required to give themselves options. Others are unwilling to sacrifice what little free time they have to invest in laying the groundwork for their escape. If you look yourself in the mirror and conclude that you (or your spouse) are not willing to make those sacrifices, then the time is not right for you to make your escape. If, however, you (and your spouse) are willing to make those sacrifices, then you would be wise to do the following: (1) minimize your monthly expenses to free up cash; (2) invest in yourself and your future (books, seminars, business coaching, mastermind groups, etc.); (3) use your excess cash to build up reserves that can cover at least twelve months of your basic monthly expenses; (4) if you are able, build up additional investment capital (above your twelve-month cash cushion), which will provide the seed capital for equity investments in real estate or other ventures; and (5) try to generate cash flow from your entrepreneurial pursuit(s) before you make your escape (in other words, create a business that actually makes money—more on this below). Again, personal finance is perhaps the most important aspect of planning. One absolutely must engage this part of the process.

- *Make the decision between an "internal" and "external" escape.* If you have followed all the steps above (as well as any others that you may identify along the way), then you are ready to make the decision about whether to escape the traditional path and, if so, whether it will be "internal" or "external." An internal escape is one where the individual continues to practice law, but gradually builds business interests outside of it. The goal of an internal escape is to build streams of cash flow in addition to one's practice so that one day, if they desire, they can completely step away from the practice of law to manage those other business interests. The internal approach is perfect for the lawyer who truly enjoys their practice, but wants to diversify their interests and assets. It's also good for the lawyer who lacks the confidence, at least at present, to completely cut the cord. Surely, anyone who has graduated from law school, passed a bar exam, and is practicing law can do what Patrick J. McGinnis recommends in his fantastic book, *The 10% Entrepreneur*. His advice is to invest 10 percent of your time and 10 percent of your capital on new investments and opportunities.[3]

Others may decide, as I did, that an "external" escape is the only way to go. In that case, like Andy Dufresne, it is extremely important that the lawyer takes a disciplined, methodical approach to escape planning and execute their escape at the optimal time, leaving as many options open as possible.

Again, while this list is not exhaustive, it is representative of the types of questions and considerations that one must evaluate when contemplating an escape from the practice of law. This process requires transparency, honesty, and alignment of priorities, both individually and with those who will be directly impacted by one's decision to escape the practice of law.

While this process is essentially the same for those who are currently practicing law for those either considering or currently attending law school, the latter can (and should) take a slightly different approach. First, for those who may be in college and considering attending law school, this book is not at all intended to talk you out of going to law school. Unlike Sam Zell, I absolutely loved every minute of my law school experience. My wife, who is also a lawyer, makes fun of me when I say that I would go to law school again just for the intellectual fun of it. She knows it's true.

If you think you might want to practice law, or you believe that attending law school will help you develop skills and give you options, then you should by all means do so. I urge you, however, to think carefully about where you go to school and the corresponding financial commitment. I do not necessarily

---

3   There is significance to this 10 percent number, as that is also traditionally the starting point for giving in many religious traditions (i.e., the tithe), including Judaism and Christianity. There are many fantastic books on the spiritual power of tithing and giving from one's "first fruits," and I believe that power is also applicable to the process of an "internal" escape from the practice of law.

disagree with the advice most people receive, which is to go to the most prestigious school that accepts you. I would simply caution you to consider whether another law school might be less expensive or offer scholarship funds, which will reduce the cost and loans you incur, especially if you intend to make your escape to business relatively quickly. The fewer loans and other financial burdens you take on during law school, the greater freedom and flexibility you will have in the future. Another important point is to research whether the law school you are considering has any prominent alumni who have transitioned from the practice of law into a field of interest to you. You might be able to leverage your alumni network to receive mentorship, guidance or, at a minimum, a clear model on which you can base your plan.

For those who are already in law school, my advice is to not feel compelled to go into practice if you have a genuine desire to pursue another path. It seems advisable that one who goes through three years of law school should at the very least sit for a bar exam and give the practice of law a try. However, if like Jim Cramer, George Roberts, or Dan Gilbert, you have a clear vision of your path to success and it does not require or involve practicing law, then you should go for it. Many of you might cringe at the thought of telling your parents or loved ones of such a decision, but perhaps you could share the relevant Alpha profiles contained in this book to allay their fears.

As I shared in the beginning of this book, I escaped the practice of law twice. Although my first attempt failed, it was not fatal to my professional life. My plan was solid; my timing was just off. I regrouped, went back into the practice of law, continued to hone my skills, and tweaked my plan as necessary to be prepared for the next opportunity. When I went back into the practice of law, I was ready to make an internal escape and play the long game, building cash-producing assets and business interests over many years. As I earned more success within the practice of law, however, I remained unfulfilled and unsatisfied, and I realized that an external escape was the only way for me.

You must answer all these questions for yourself. Only you can design the lifestyle of your dreams and clearly define your vision of success. Only you can identify the other industries and businesses that are of interest to you and where you believe you can add value in the marketplace. Only you can honestly determine whether you are willing to make the necessary sacrifices and willing to accept the risks that you will absolutely have to endure to overcome obstacles along the way. There are no objectively right answers to these questions, but to responsibly determine whether you are ready to escape the practice of law, you have no choice but to answer them.

CHAPTER THIRTEEN
For Those Who Remain

---

t is entirely possible that after reading this book, you have determined that practicing law is exactly where you should be. You may have determined that you truly enjoy the practice of law. While there may be a few things you would change to earn more money or derive more joy from your profession, your definition of success does not require that you escape the practice of law. Perhaps you have discovered that you want to become an entrepreneur within the practice of law, not outside of it.

If you have reached that conclusion, I commend you and would be truly humbled if this book played any role in helping you come to that realization. Nevertheless, I have some suggestions for how you could perhaps bring an entrepreneurial focus and mindset to your practice and produce even greater joy and satisfaction.

It is no secret that the legal industry is at the very beginning stages of massive disruption. Technology is increasingly being leveraged to perform tasks (for example, discovery services) that lawyers were once able to perform for clients at the rate of hundreds of dollars per hour. Corporations and other consumers of legal services are turning to artificial intelligence and machine learning to increase efficiency and reduce their legal costs across the board. For example, in 2016, JPMorgan Chase & Co. launched a new software program called COIN ("**Contract Intelligence**") that performs the important tasks of analyzing and interpreting commercial loan agreements. Until the bank transitioned to this technology, it was estimated this work generated more than 300,000 billable hours each year. If one conservatively assumes a rate of $300/hour to perform those services, this single innovation resulted in the loss of nearly $100 million of billable revenue (or expense, depending on one's perspective) in the blink of an eye.

The COIN initiative is but one example of disruptive technology targeting traditional legal services. Industry publications, such as *The American Lawyer*, are replete with almost daily stories about cutting-edge technology targeting rote tasks typically performed by lawyers, such as a machine learning application called "Lia" deployed by Allstate Insurance Company to answer routine legal questions from its various business units. With respect to legal services themselves, a cutting-edge law firm called Atrium touts a technology platform called Legal Technology Services to complete financing transactions for venture-backed startups. Blockchain technology has the promise of providing a cryptographic platform for certain types of contracts and international transactions in the very near future. As the legendary venture capital investor Marc Andreesen has observed, we can no longer avoid the fact that "software is eating the world," and the legal profession is definitely not exempt.

Although disruption is real and already underway, this does not mean that the need for quality legal services performed by sentient beings will entirely disappear. Clients will continue to demand legal expertise performed by high-quality, creative lawyers who can evaluate and adapt to aspects of complex matters that (at least for the foreseeable future) technology is not optimized to perform. The caveat, however, is that those clients will demand efficiency and the market will drive the price of legal services accordingly. This means those services that can and should be performed by leveraging technology will be priced much lower than those that rely on the true expertise and value that human beings and law firms can provide. Services such as creative arguments, solutions, and pattern recognition that enable those individuals and firms to anticipate a client's needs and steer them away from troubled waters, or toward lucrative opportunities could still command a premium.

As such, I believe that two segments of the law firm market will thrive in this new paradigm, and one will be decimated. The two that will thrive are international "mega" law firms on the one hand, and niche-focused, boutique law firms on the other. The segment that I believe will struggle is the mid-market regional firm, meaning those that are "full-service" law firms with anywhere from fifty to several hundred lawyers and even more support staff. While I could certainly be wrong about this, I sincerely believe this is inevitable.

The international mega firms will survive and grow because large, global companies will require highly skilled lawyers to efficiently represent them in connection with high-stakes litigation, intellectual property, and corporate matters, among other engagements. Also, those firms will be highly incentivized and have the means to invest in technology to profitably augment their legal services. Conversely, regional, full-service firms will either be snapped up by international mega firms, split up into smaller niche-focused firms, or will be forced to dissolve. Their overhead structures and rosters of highly paid, underperforming partners and senior associates make it increasingly difficult to earn enough business and revenue to feed the machine, let alone make the investments in technology and non-lawyer technology experts to compete with the mega firms (with respect to scale and expertise) or the boutiques (with respect to price).

This leaves the third category, comprised of smaller, niche-focused boutique firms. The bleak picture painted above for the mid-market regional firms creates a massive opportunity for entrepreneurially minded and technologically savvy lawyers and law firms. If you have reached this chapter and are more committed than ever to being an entrepreneur within the legal services industry, then perhaps now is the time to branch out and start a niche-focused, boutique law firm on your own or with a handful of likeminded partners.

As this market shift takes hold, the international mega firms will focus their efforts on the largest clients with "bet-the-company" legal matters that are likely to produce the largest fees. This means a huge, profitable swath of the market (i.e., lower middle market, middle market, and scale-up companies) will be up for grabs. Those clients will gravitate toward lawyers and firms that have the desired legal expertise, but can also be more creative with pricing and fee structures by leveraging technology and reducing overhead (by not having as many attorneys, support staff, or overly fancy office space). There will also be opportunities for creative niche firms to collaborate with experts in other niche practice areas to deliver solutions for clients with diverse needs without formally combining into one firm.

For one to be successful and happy practicing law in this new paradigm, he must be entrepreneurially minded and bring the principles of efficiency, strategy, and growth to the practice of law. While the practice of law will continue to be viewed as a profession (as it should), with the expectation that those who practice will maintain the highest ethical standards, in order to thrive the firm of the future must also be viewed by its owners and its clients as a business. Legal entrepreneurs must look beyond the outdated framework provided by the American Bar Association, state bar associations, and other old-school "how to start a law firm" resources to develop best practices for starting and scaling the profitable law firm of the future.

Through my own legal practice, as well as during my time as an investment banker, investor, and strategic consultant, I have observed that the most successful companies and those that command a premium upon exit are also the most disciplined and focused when it comes to operations. Specifically, all the companies that I have worked with that have implemented the "Scaling Up" business operating system (also known as the Rockefeller Habits, which are detailed in the books of the same names by business thinker Verne Harnish) have been, by far, more efficient and profitable than their peers in the relevant market. This has been validated by the many strategic and private equity buyers that have acquired those companies and paid a premium for the turnkey nature of those businesses. Personally, I was so convinced that the Scaling Up system was responsible for these results that I applied the principles as I was growing my law practice, and we consistently apply them in our businesses today.[4]

It doesn't matter whether you are considering or currently attending law school, or already practicing law and you see the impending disruption coming down the pike. If you are going to continue to practice law and you have the passion and drive to build your own practice, now is the perfect time to start your own firm. Some of the same considerations that we discussed in Chapters Eleven and Twelve will equally apply to the process of starting your own firm. You must begin with the end in mind and articulate, in vivid detail, your vision for success and your ideal lifestyle. Then, you must diligently order your affairs, including your personal finances, and go through the process of setting up your firm. Once you launch the firm, you should then run it and scale it like a real business. Done properly, the firm should serve you rather than become your master.

---

4   In short, the Scaling Up operating system focuses on four key issues that every leader must address when scaling his business: (1) attracting and keeping the right *people*; (2) creating a truly differentiated *strategy* when compared to competitors; (3) driving flawless *execution* of that strategy; and (4) ensuring that the business and the entrepreneur have plenty of *cash* to weather the storms that will inevitably arise along the path from scale up to exit.

CHAPTER FOURTEEN

Conclusion

———

Over the last thirteen chapters, we have studied the lives of nearly sixty lawyers who transitioned to entrepreneurship in a variety of fields, and we reviewed the steps one must take to mount a successful escape from the practice of law or build an entrepreneurial law firm of the future. While several Alphas started their own law firms and others pursued their escape in the same industry (real estate, private equity, etc.), no two paths to success were the same. These men and women each faced adversity at points along their journey and made measurable sacrifices to accomplish their goals. While it is safe to say that most (if not all) of them set out on their journey seeking maximum personal freedom, as opposed to simply more money, they each earned tremendous wealth along the way.

As previously noted, the message of this book is not, "Do these things and you too can become a billionaire." Rather, my sincere hope is that this book will free your mind to consider the possibilities in your life. That you will face and dismiss fears that have been holding you back. And that, regardless of whether you decide to go for it and escape the practice of law, or redouble your efforts and build a profitable and scalable law practice, you will be purposeful and deliberately design and pursue the lifestyle that perfectly suits you. My hope is that you will be deliberate about defining success and then go after it with everything you have.

Thank you for taking the time to read this, and I hope that some piece of this book has been or will be of service to you on your journey.

ACKNOWLEDGEMENTS

have been passionate about writing for a long time, but this is my first attempt at publishing a full-length work. So many people have helped me throughout my life and, in doing so, played a part in making this book possible. I am truly humbled to have the opportunity to thank them on these pages.

In particular, I would like to thank the following people:

To the team at Morgan James Publishing, thank you for your belief in this project and the immense support you have provided.

To my editor, Lisa Cerasoli, thank you for your patience and enthusiasm as we turned the manuscript into a finished work.

To all of my teachers and professors throughout the years, who saw things in me and encouraged me well before I had confidence in myself or my abilities. Specifically, I thank: Mrs. Verona Grady, my elementary school teacher, who introduced me to the first personal computer I ever used and sparked a passion for learning new things; Mr. Ross Kershey, my Honors History teacher, who made history come alive and taught me the value of spirited debate; Mr. James Hudson, my AP English teacher and the man who stoked my passion for reading, writing, and thinking; Father Anthony Ugolnik, my college professor, mentor, and dear friend, a man who demonstrated that there is no greater love than to lay down one's life for others; Professor David Josephson, who challenged and supported me in so many ways; and Professor Patrick Johnston, my law school professor who has always treated me as a peer and encouraged me to pursue my dreams.

To all of my mentors, partners and colleagues in the practice of law, specifically: the late Justice Joseph Walsh, Mark Morton, Michael Tumas, John

Grossbauer, Mike Pittenger, Scott Waxman, Rick Cross, Chris Simon, Matt Greenberg, Barry Levin, Wendy Stabler, Bill Manning, Bill Gee, Jim Taylor, Mark Minuti, Richard Forsten, Dan Krapf, Terry Currier, Rick Carroll, Debbie Spranger, Eric Orlinsky, Adam Zarren, Adam Kelson, Matt Draper, Stan Kull, David Shapiro, David Antzis, and Joe O'Dea. And especially to: Catherine Strickler Gaul, Mike Reilly, and Jim Tobia, my Potter Anderson "crew" in the early days—thank you for being good friends and for making me laugh with your gallows humor. And to Lynanne B. Wescott, the late Jim Kilcur, and Jim Keller, who were the first people to demonstrate to me what it really means to be a lawyer—this book never would have happened without you.

To the writers and thinkers who helped me realize that I could do this, specifically Tim Ferriss, Ryan Holiday, Jocko Wilink, Gary Vaynerchuck, James Altucher, Rich Roll and Jon Acuff.

To my friends Joe Miller and Stephanie Madoff Mack, who read early drafts of this book and provided valuable, independent feedback.

To Katie Garvey, our babysitter, lacrosse coach, and intern extraordinaire, whose research, editing, and enthusiasm helped me get this project over the finish line. I know that you are destined for great things!

To my partner and colleagues at align5, John Ratliff, Denise Richmond, and Beth Dietrich. Your support and friendship mean the world to me. You make the adventure fun!

To my parents, Tom and SueAnn Williams, my siblings, Laura Williams and Rick Leith, Allison and Jared Colligan, and Trevor and Heidi Williams; Cara's parents, Tom and Sue Fanelli, and her siblings, Alicia, Tommy, and Denise Fanelli; as well as our grandparents, nieces, nephews, aunts, uncles, cousins, and my lifelong friends. Your love and support throughout my life instilled in me the passion and drive to pursue my dreams.

To my dog, Winston, who lay at my feet or had his head on my lap during most of the researching, writing, and editing of this book. I am so thankful for his companionship.

To my children, Tatum, Marin, Charlie, and Taylor. Your love propels me forward each day. I pray I will continue to inspire each of you to live a life of your own design.

To my wife, Cara. You are the smartest, kindest, and hardest working woman I know. I realize that I am a challenging person to live with, and I am so grateful that you've stuck with me! Thank you for your unconditional love, support, and friendship as we continue to design our lives together. I love you with all of my heart.

ABOUT THE AUTHOR

Chad Williams is an entrepreneur, advisor, investor, writer, and former partner in an AmLaw 200 law firm. His company, align5, is a strategic consulting and boutique investment banking firm that works with growth company entrepreneurs as they scale their businesses and prepare to maximize value upon exit. Chad also works with entrepreneurial lawyers to help them apply the scaling-up principles to both their law practices, as well as their business interests outside of the law. He lives outside of Philadelphia, Pennsylvania, with his wife, four children, and two dogs.

bridgeacademy
& community center

The author is donating a portion of the profits generated by this book to the Bridge Academy and Community Center.

The Bridge Academy & Community Center provides a safe and loving environment for children and families in Coatesville, Pennsylvania. Its mission is to equip youth and families with the tools necessary for academic achievement, life skills, creative expression, spiritual growth and leadership.

For more information on Bridge Academy, please visit
www.thebridgeacademy.org

Morgan James
Speakers Group

We connect Morgan James published authors with live and online events and audiences who will benefit from their expertise.

Morgan James makes all of our titles available
through the Library for All Charity Organization.

www.LibraryForAll.org

Printed in the USA
CPSIA information can be obtained
at www.ICGtesting.com
JSHW022341140824
68134JS00019B/1615